Real iOS App Development

A Sample-Code Approach to Building Apps

Dale Matheny

Real iOS App Development is an independent publication and has not been authorized, sponsored, or otherwise approved by Apple Inc. Apple, iTunes Store, iPhone, iPad are registered trademarks of Apple Inc. registered in the U.S. and other countries.

Duck Feet image from Game Inc., used by permission, July 2015.

Contents

Real iOS App Development

Chapter 1: Getting Started

This book will teach you how to create iOS apps by giving you the complete code of a powerful App Store app. The book guides you through the code of this app, called **WebMarks**, step-by-step. The app starts simple but gains in power until it becomes a real-world app that allows collaborative data exchange among hundreds of users. The app is on the App Store so you can download it. There is also a website for this book that contains a complete, ready-to-run, code project of the complete app at www.RayOfLightSoftware.com/WebMarks.

This book uses Xcode 6 or higher for iOS version 8.0 or later as the Apple development environment and Objective C++ as the coding language (versus Swift which is a new language developed by Apple). You can learn Objective C++ by studying the code if you already know a programming language.

Building the app will reveal how to build iOS apps in general and give you a starter app and code segments for common functions that you can copy into your own apps. After building the app in this book you will need to build your own app, reusing the provided code segments, to get the material under your belt. An excellent iOS and mobile app user interface guide from Apple is available at: https://developer.apple.com/library/ios/documentation/UserExperience/Conceptual/MobileHIG

Chapters 1-7 take you through the **basics and fundamental screens and navigational tools** to build an app: Tab and Navigation Bars, Simple Views, Table Views and Web Views. Chapter 6 covers testing techniques and can be read and used at any time!

Chapters 8 – 11 are more advanced and deal with **data storage in local and remote databases and server calls**. These are power features that many books don't cover but are important to add powerful 'real app' features and capabilities to your app. Chapter 11 gives a detailed overview of what it takes to create shared data applications with the creation of a Group concept: users can store data in protected groups where only users with access rights can see or share data. This feature makes this app into a social bookmark app!

Chapter 12 gives a short introduction to **integration** with iOS libraries to easily use **social sharing** features such as Email, Facebook, and Twitter. Chapter 13 gives you a tutorial on adding iAds, Apples' advertisments, within your app. Chapter 14 wraps up the app by showing how to add icons and **submit apps to the App Store**.

Building apps is very empowering. Enjoy!

Symbols used in this book

The symbols below are critical to guiding you through the book quickly.

This is an **action** step to build the sample app. This if a step for you to do and usually includes copying (or typing) code or other commands within the XCODE IDE (Integrated Development Environment. Code to add will appear with a grey background. Code with a white background is existing code and is not be added.

Example below, only add the code for the one row "return 1;".

```
- (NSInteger)numberOfSectionsInTableView:(UITableView *)tableView {
    // Return the number of sections.
    return 1;
}
```

Code comments are given by matching arrow icons as shown. The icon appears next to the code and then below the code the corresponding letter gives a description of that code.

Run the sample application to test it. Make sure at this step to get the app running as it should to that point and debug anything that didn't work. To debug you'll need to retrace all the action steps and ensure modifications were done exactly as specified.

Exercise. This is an additional exercise you can do to deepen your grasp of app building.

The Sample App

The sample app that is the basis of this book's exercises provides a wealth of sample code from a real application on the App Store that you can use in your own apps. The app is named *WebMarks* and is a collaborative bookmark app for websites. It is meant to demonstrate all topics in this book including all basic view types used in apps and data usage within an app and using both local and remote databases.

Web-based data

When data is stored on a remote server you have created a collaborative app that allows anyone in the world with the app to exchange and share information—this is the most powerful ability of apps and is usually *not* covered in beginning texts but, in the end, is a fairly straightforward capability that you can master. This capability separates a hobby from a professional app and gives the app much broader potential for functionality and income.

Downloading the development environment and sample app code

Download the free iOS app development environment, XCODE, from Apple via the Mac App Store application. There is no charge to *develop* apps. When you *distribute* an app you need to be an official Apple Developer which costs $99/year.

Book Website: **www.rayoflightsoftware.com/WebMarks**

1. Download the folder "WebMarks_Book" to your Desktop by clicking on the "Download Book Support Files" button. It has all the sample code you'll need for this book to learn app building and to use in building your own app as well as other supporting files.
2. If you've got the print book you'll want to be sure to the file: Real iOS App Development Code File.rtf that is included in the WebMarks_Book files. It contains all of the code in this book in an easy format to copy and paste.
3. To ensure XCode has the appropriate starter app template in it, copy and paste the folder "Empty Application.xctemplate" from the WebMarks_Book folder you downloaded into the path below using the Go/Go To Folder menu option in the Finder application on your Mac:

/Applications/Xcode.app/Contents/Developer/Platforms/iPhoneOS.platform/Developer/ Library/Xcode/Templates/Project Templates/iOS/Application

All of the code in this book is provided license free and can be freely used within your own apps with the *limitation that you cannot redistribute the WebMarks app, or the majority thereof, in any form or under a different name.*

The Development Environment

1 Go into the sites_sample folder and double-click the file: ***sites.xcodeproj***, this is the app project file, and opens the app project.

The developer environment loads as shown below. Note the icons above the project file list:

- the left folder icon takes you to the project file list
- the search icon allows you to search all code for a string
- and the exclamation point icon takes you to a list of errors if the compile and build of the application doesn't work.

The icons on the right open and close the project, code, and properties panels within the XCode development environment. Experiment with each of these.

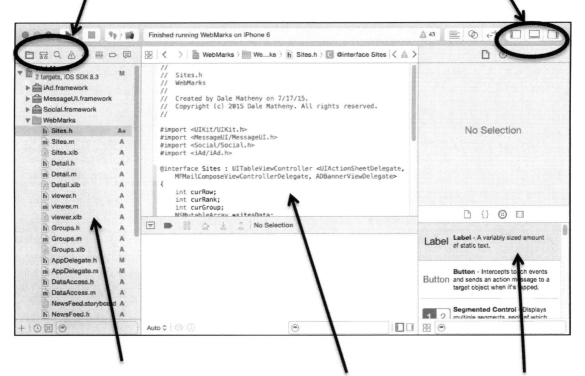

On the left is the WebMarks project folder and all subfolders. All of the source code, screen resources, and image files are contained here.

The middle panel is where code appears and debug information when the code is running appears below it.

Properties on the right panel.

Run the Sample App in the Simulator

Pick a simulator device (iPhone 5, 6, iPad, etc.) and press the run arrow in the upper left. The app will run in the separate simulator program provided by Apple. Wait for the app to appear in the simulator—it's a bit slow the first time. **Explore!**

The app has 20+ functions that you can use to build many other apps.

A **TabBar** (a main navigational construct in iOS) is at the bottom of the screen and shows two main screens in the app: The WebMarks screen uses a **Table View** which displays a list of items and is the main type of screen in use in iOS apps. This screen contains website links that you'll be able to browse in the second screen, the web Browser which is of type **Web View** (one of several main screen types in iOS).

Chapter 2: Create the Project

This section walks through creating the sample App, *Sites*.

Select the **File, New Project** menu item. Select **Empty Application**, press **Next**.

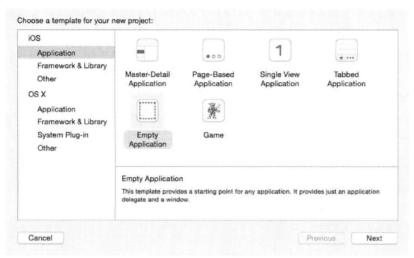

Type a name of **WebMarks** and press **Next**. Press **Create** on the directory screen after telling the system what parent folder you wish to store your application.

XCODE will create a WebMarks code folder on your disk drive where you tell it to and all files for your application project will be placed in this folder. You will sometimes need to manually add files to this folder so go to finder after its created and make sure you can find it.

Creating Screens

This is your main development environment. All project files are in a finder like tree on the left.

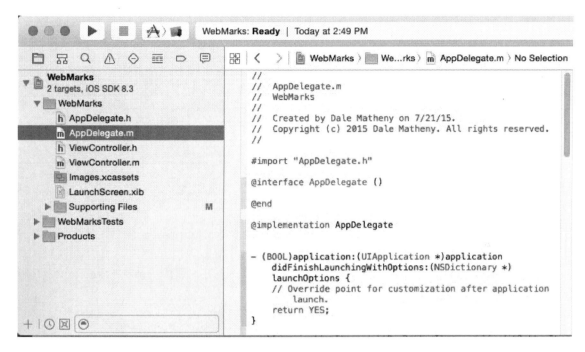

The AppDelegate .h and .m files is the main application object that controls the app and the first screen opened. We now create new screens used in the app.

Select **File / New / File ...** menu. You will see this screen. Click on "Cocoa Touch Class" and then **Next**.

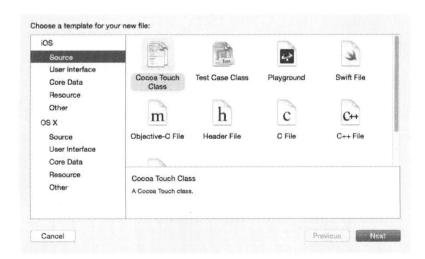

4 Type class name **Sites** which is a subclass of **UITableViewController** and check "**Also create XIB file**". The XIB is a screen file we can use in the User Interface builder. Press **Next** and then press **Create.**

5 Repeat the steps to create a **UIViewController** with the name of **Detail** (capitalization is important) and make sure to **include an XIB file**. Note this is a UIViewController not a UITableViewController like we selected for the Sites screen above.

We want to copy three files from the directory: viewer.h, viewer.m and viewer.xib into the Sites project folder. To do this open Finder, navigate to the folder:

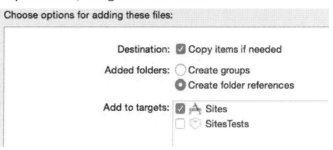

WebMarks_Books and drag/drop the viewer files into the new project screen. Alternatively right-click on the *WebMarks* project and select "Add Files…" and select the files. You will see a screen as follows and be sure to check the option "Copy items if needed".

 We don't need the empty application's default view files so let us remove them. Within the project file list select both **viewcontroller.h and viewcontroller.m,** the and right-click and select **Delete**. Select the option: "Move to Trash".

The image to the right shows all the new files (screens) you just created. The *AppDelegate* main app starting class (code) and most of the screens we will have in the app: *Sites, Detail, and viewer.*

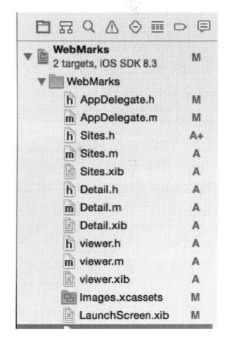

Chapter 3: Navigation using TabBar and Navigation Bar

Tab Bar's and Navigation bars are the two fundamental navigational techniques within apps. The Sites sample app uses both approaches and they are set up within the AppDelegate main app function when the application first runs.

Setting the root screen in AppDelegate.m

 Copy in all code in the grey boxes below to the AppDelegate.m files. Code should already be in the files so copy and paste the italicized code only from this document to the code files. To open the files, single click on them in the project file list.

To understand the logic, read the code documentation which follows the // comment symbol or within /* ...comments... */ comment blocks.

The import statements below are at the top of the AppDelegate.m code file and include the header file(s) (object definition files) for objects referenced in code.

```
#import "AppDelegate.h"
#import "Sites.h"
#import "viewer.h"
```

The interface section adds a new object property (variable) for our navigation type which is a tabBarController—the bar of icons at the bottom of the app.

```
@interface AppDelegate ()
@property (strong, nonatomic) UITabBarController *tabBarController;
@end
```

The *Implementation* section below holds all of the methods for AppDelegate. Copy the code below into the iOS supplied method ***didFinishLaunchingWithOptions*** as follows. This method is called once when the app is launched by a user. The code below creates and adds two screens to the *tabBarController* object.

```
@implementation AppDelegate
-(BOOL)application:(UIApplication *)application didFinishLaunchingWithOptions:(NSDictionary
*)launchOptions {
    self.window = [[UIWindow alloc] initWithFrame:[[UIScreen mainScreen] bounds]];
    //Creates two view controller pointers for the two screens in the Tab Bar

    UIViewController *viewController1;
    viewer *viewController2;

    //Creates the Sites screen
    viewController1 = [[Sites alloc] initWithNibName:@"Sites" bundle:nil];

    //Creates the web view screen
```

```
        viewController2 = [[viewer alloc] initWithNibName:@"viewer" bundle:nil];
        viewController2.Url=[NSURL URLWithString:@"http://www.google.com"];
        viewController2.navigationItem.title=@"Browser";

        //Creates the main navigational construct: TabBar as a UITabBarController subclass

        self.tabBarController = [[UITabBarController alloc] init];
        self.tabBarController.tabBar.tintColor = [UIColor colorWithRed:0.0 green:0.212 blue:0.416
alpha:1.0];

        //Create an array to hold both screens within the TabBar
        NSMutableArray *localViewControllersArray = [[NSMutableArray alloc] initWithCapacity:2];

        //Sites screen added within a NavigationController to the TabBar

        UINavigationController *theNavigationController;
        theNavigationController = [[UINavigationController alloc]
initWithRootViewController:viewController1];
        [localViewControllersArray addObject:theNavigationController];

        //NewsFeed screen added within a NavigationController to the TabBar
        theNavigationController = [[UINavigationController alloc]
initWithRootViewController:viewController2];
        [localViewControllersArray addObject:theNavigationController];
        viewController2.tabBarItem.image = [UIImage imageNamed:@"web"];
        viewController2.title = NSLocalizedString(@"Browser", @"Browser");

        //Bring it all together.  Hook up the view controllers to the tab bar and the tabBar as the root
view controller for the entire app by hooking it to the app window rootViewController
        self.tabBarController.viewControllers=localViewControllersArray;
        self.window.rootViewController = self.tabBarController;
        self.window.backgroundColor = [UIColor whiteColor];
        [self.window makeKeyAndVisible];

    return YES;
}
```

A Create two screens (viewControllers): Sites and viewer.

B Create the *tabBarController* which has 2 tabs. Later in the code, the viewControllers or screens get assigned to the tabBarController and the tabBarController is assigned as the rootViewController which is the root object of the application that all other screens 'hang' off of.

C A navigation controller is created for each screen and the screen (viewController) is assigned as its root. Navigation controllers provide a hierarchy or stack of screens that can be used to 'drill' into a screen and then pop back out to the root.

The code above should be broken down and studied—a lot is happening that is critical to understanding how an application is structured, including its navigation and screens. The examples here can be used to create your own apps that use one or more screens linked to a TabBar or Navigation Controllers.

Question: To add a third screen to the app, what would you change?
Answer: You would need another viewController like this:

UIViewController *viewController1, *viewController3;

And then initialize that viewController with something similar to this:

viewController1 = [[Sites alloc] initWithNibName:@"XIBofMyThirdScreen" bundle:nil];

And then add that viewController3 object to the TabBar like this:
theNavigationController = [[UINavigationController alloc]
initWithRootViewController:viewController1];
[localViewControllersArray addObject:theNavigationController];

You would also need to change the *localViewControllersArray* capacity from 2 to 3. In the end, you have a new screen in your TabBar. Cool stuff!

Add the following code to set the Sites screen title and tabbar icon. Add it to the Sites.m file at the top.

@implementation Sites

```
- (id)initWithNibName:(NSString *)nibNameOrNil bundle:(NSBundle *)nibBundleOrNil
{
    self = [super initWithNibName:nibNameOrNil bundle:nibBundleOrNil];
    if (self) {
        self.title = NSLocalizedString(@"WebMarks", @"WebMarks");
        self.tabBarItem.image = [UIImage imageNamed:@"link"];
    }

    return self;
}
```

Now add icons (images) to your app by opening, in Finder, the folder WebMarks_Book/Images. Drag and drop all .png image files to the project file area in XCode. A dialog will appear for the copy and be sure to check "ON" the option *"Copy items if needed"* to make sure you copy (not just reference) the icon files into your application source code folder. Note that the *link* and *web* images will be used by code we just added.

Run the app! To run the app in the iPhone simulator press the right arrow at the top of the XCODE development environment as shown below. You can also select the device the simulator runs the app in by clicking on the "iPhone 6" icon and select a device such iPhone 6 (or iPhone 5, etc).

The screen will appear as in the image to the right with the two tabs, "WebMarks" and "Browser" appearing with icons. WebMarks screen corresponds to our *Sites* code files and Browser is our *viewer* files.

Study how the structure of this app was put together and then create a new app and try it on your own. Create two or three screens and attach them to a TabBar and make sure you understand this critical step of creating apps!

Chapter 4: Table views

A UITableView contains a list of information and is one of the most used screen types in apps.

The implementation of the screen is divided between code for displaying and interacting with the list of cells of information and code to maintain the underlying data that supports the list. This section gets the Sites tableview working which will display a list of websites that we save. Remember to study the code to learn Objective-C++ if you don't already know it.

Local app data storage

To be able to display a list of data we must first create the data to be displayed in an Objective C++ array data structure: the *NSMutableArray* data object. The NSMutableArray is flexible because *mutable* means it can flex in size dynamically, even after the object is first created. The *sitesData* NSMutableArray below contains all rows of data to be displayed in the UITableView (list) and each array element of sites represents one website and one row in the list. To be specific, *sitesData* is an array of *NSDictionary* class objects, each of which contains a set of data elements that define a website: its name, URL, etc.

sitesData is an array of NSDictionarys which hold 'value pairs'—each pair has a value followed by its field name. The example below of sitesData has two NSDIctionary objects each with 6 value pairs. The row 0 of the array has first pair of "id" with value=1, "name" with value "CNN", etc.

0	1,"id"	"CNN", "name"	"http://www.cnn.com","site"	0,"rank"	0,"owner"	"", "attributes"
1	1,"id"	"CNN", "name"	"http://www.cnn.com","site"	0,"rank"	0,"owner"	"", "attributes"

Sites.h

The Sites.h header file needs to define two objects: our *sitesData* mutable array and a default (empty) website which is single NSDictionary element.

```objc
#import <UIKit/UIKit.h>
@interface Sites : UITableViewController
{
    NSMutableArray *sitesData;
    NSDictionary *default_site;
}

@property (nonatomic, retain) NSDictionary *default_site;
@property (nonatomic,strong) NSMutableArray * sitesData;

@end
```

Sites.m

All code goes in the .m file (.m for Methods).

```
@implementation Sites
@synthesize default_site,sitesData;

- (void)viewDidLoad {
    [super viewDidLoad];
```

```
    default_site=[[NSDictionary alloc] initWithObjectsAndKeys:[NSNumber
numberWithInt:0],@"id",@"", @"name",@"",@"site",[NSNumber
numberWithInt:0],@"rank",@"",@"attributes",nil];
    [self manualLoad];   // Local Objection C++ data structures -- non-persistent

    // Uncomment the following line to preserve selection between presentations.
    // self.clearsSelectionOnViewWillAppear = NO;

    // Uncomment the following line to display an Edit button in the navigation bar for this view
controller.
}

-(void)manualLoad {
    if (self.sitesData==nil)
        self.sitesData = [NSMutableArray new];
    else {
        [self.sitesData removeAllObjects];
    }
```

```
    NSDictionary *row1=[[NSDictionary alloc] initWithObjectsAndKeys:[NSNumber
numberWithInt:100], @"id",@"CNN",@"name",@"http://www.CNN.com",@"site", [NSNumber
numberWithInt:3], @"rank",@"",@"attrbiutes",nil];
    [self.sitesData addObject:row1];

    row1=[[NSDictionary alloc] initWithObjectsAndKeys:[NSNumber numberWithInt:100],
@"id",@"Christian Science Monitor",@"name",@"http://www.csmonitor.com",@"site", [NSNumber
numberWithInt:4], @"rank",@"",@"attrbiutes",nil];
    [self.sitesData addObject:row1];
}
```

Here we initialize the default_site NSDictionary object with default values. Note an NSDictionary is a set of data pairs. Each pair is the data object followed by a NSString textual tag for the data. Example: @"", @"name" below sets the name field to a value of empty string—this is one data/tag pair in the NSDictionary. The method numberWithInt converts an integer into a NSNumber object since NSDictionaries require object values. NSString's are objects already so the @"CNN" type of strings used are string objects.

Set the first two rows of default website data so we can get our TableView running in the following section. Note the method *addObject*: is the code that adds each website (NSDictionary object named *row1*) to the *sitesData* array. By the end of the code, *sitesData* array has 2 NSDictionry objects (2 websites) defined in it.

TableView: Displaying Data

There are three standard--provided by XCode--methods of a UITableView that must be implemented to provide the list functionality: *numberOfSectionsInTableView*, *numberOfRowsInSection* and *cellForRowAtIndexPath*

The *cellForRowAtIndexPath* method is the most important method as it gets called by the system once for each row to display the list—ie, it gets called *numberOfRowsInSection* times. A standard list only has one section and so most of the time *numberOfSectionsInTableView* returns 1.

```
#pragma mark - Table view data source

- (NSInteger)numberOfSectionsInTableView:(UITableView *)tableView {
    // Return the number of sections.
    return 1;
}
```

Below, replace the code "return 0" in the method *numberOfRowsInSection* with what is in grey below:

```
- (NSInteger)tableView:(UITableView *)tableView numberOfRowsInSection:(NSInteger)section {
    // Return the number of rows in the section by using the NSMutableArray's count method
    return [self.sitesData count];

;
```

```
- (CGFloat)tableView:(UITableView *)tableView heightForRowAtIndexPath:(NSIndexPath
*)indexPath
{
    return 50;
}
```

Uncomment the *cellForRowAtIndexPath* method by removing the /* and */ comment blocks and replace the code in the method with the code in grey below.

```
- (UITableViewCell *)tableView:(UITableView *)tableView
cellForRowAtIndexPath:(NSIndexPath *)indexPath {
    //cell is an object that holds all data to display for a row
    static NSString *CellIdentifier = @"Cell";
    UITableViewCell *cell = [tableView dequeueReusableCellWithIdentifier:CellIdentifier];
    if (cell == nil) {
        cell = [[UITableViewCell alloc] initWithStyle:UITableViewCellStyleSubtitle
reuseIdentifier:CellIdentifier];
    }

    // Configure the cell data textLabel and detailTextLabel from data within the sites data objects.
```

Note the objectAtIndex pulls out a NSDictionary object into rowdata for the current website we want to display

```
    NSDictionary *rowdata = [self.sitesData objectAtIndex:indexPath.row];
    cell.textLabel.text = [rowdata objectForKey:@"name"];
    cell.detailTextLabel.text = [rowdata objectForKey:@"site"];
    cell.accessoryType = UITableViewCellAccessoryDetailDisclosureButton;

    //Place duck feet icon on row
    NSString *path = [[NSBundle mainBundle] pathForResource:@"Duck29" ofType:@"png"];
    UIImage *theImage = [UIImage imageWithContentsOfFile:path];
    cell.imageView.image = theImage;

        return cell;
}
```

[self.sitesData count] returns the number of records in sitesData. Count is a method of the NSMutableData object the returns the count property.

heightForRowAtIndexPath is an optional method that we use to change the row height of each row in the UITableView. In our case we set the height of each row to 60 pixels.

The parameter *indexPath.row* (which starts at zero and increments up to the returned value in the function *numberOfRowsInSection*) stores the row that will be displayed. Note that the variable rowdata is of type *NSDictionary* and we load it with the current (indexPath.row) row of data from the *sitesData* array. We then access data elements from rowdata using the method **objectForKey**:@"[key]" where key is name, site, etc.

You can now run the app again by pressing the 'Play' icon in the upper left corner of XCode. You should see a complete WebMarks screen with two default (and famous! newspaper) websites: CNN and The Christian Science Monitor.

If you see the screen to the right, your UITableView is working and this is a huge step in building an app as this table (really a list) construct is the most used view type in iOS apps.

TableView: Editing

Table views allow delete, move, and add capability for cell editing. The following codes adds these editing features to Sites. The screen with editing turned *on* will look like the screen to the right. Note the last row is converted to an empty row where the user can tap "Add" to add a row.

 Add the following code within the Sites.m file.

As the last line of *viewDidLoad* uncomment the code line below that places an Edit button in the top right of the Sites screen.

```
// Uncomment the following line to display an Edit button in the navigation bar for this view controller.
        self.navigationItem.rightBarButtonItem = self.editButtonItem;
}
```

Following the *heightForRowAtIndexPath* method insert the following routines that allow editing in a tableView:

```
#pragma mark - Table view editing

// ******************************************************
// ******** TABLE EDITING LOGIC          **********
// ******************************************************

- (void)setEditing:(BOOL)editing animated:(BOOL)animate
{
    [super setEditing:editing animated:animate];
    [self.tableView reloadData];

    if(editing)
    {
        NSLog(@"edit mode on");
    }
    else
    {
        NSLog(@"leave edit mode");
    }
}

// Override to support editing the table view.
-(void)tableView:(UITableView *)tableView
commitEditingStyle:(UITableViewCellEditingStyle)editingStyle forRowAtIndexPath:(NSIndexPath
*)indexPath {

    if (editingStyle == UITableViewCellEditingStyleDelete)
```

```
      {
         [self.sitesData removeObjectAtIndex:indexPath.row];
       [tableView deleteRowsAtIndexPaths:@[indexPath]
         withRowAnimation:UITableViewRowAnimationFade];
      }

      else if (editingStyle == UITableViewCellEditingStyleInsert)
      {
          [self.sitesData insertObject:default_site atIndex:[self.sitesData count]];
          [self.tableView reloadData];
      }
   }

-(UITableViewCellEditingStyle)tableView:(UITableView *)aTableView
editingStyleForRowAtIndexPath:(NSIndexPath *)indexPath {

      // No editing style if not editing or the index path is nil.
      if (indexPath.row == [self.sitesData count]) {
          return UITableViewCellEditingStyleInsert;
      } else {
          return UITableViewCellEditingStyleDelete;
      }
      return UITableViewCellEditingStyleNone;
   }
   s
   // Override to support rearranging the table view.
   - (void)tableView:(UITableView *)tableView moveRowAtIndexPath:(NSIndexPath
   *)fromIndexPath toIndexPath:(NSIndexPath *)toIndexPath {
   }
```

Code comments:

setEditing gets called when the edit button is tapped. The routine redisplays the
TableView with the editing symbols turned on (or off) when the Edit button is toggled.
Note the format of an if statement in Objective C:

```
if( expression  ) {
        code-block
}
else
{
        code-block
}
```

The *commitEditingStyle* method performs the delete or insert of a row in the
TableView. The logic to do this is that the sites table is updated (a row removed or the
default_site row added using the methods: *removeObjectAtIndex* or *insertObject*).

The *editingStyleForRowAtIndexPath* method asks the program to return if the indexPath.row parameter passed to the routine is a row that allows an insert or delete. The constant UITableViewCellEditingStyleInsert is returned if the current row is the last row (indexPath.row == [self.sitesData count]) or returns UITableViewCellEditingStyleDelete for the other rows. We will allow adding a row if the row is the last one in the list.

 The method *moveRowAtIndexPath* has been uncommented to show you how moves occur but the routine would need to have logic added to rearrange the websites in the sitesData array to fully implement the move logic.

Now, we need to modify the display of the tableView because a bottom "Add" row will be added to the list so the user can add new rows. This row is a special row and doesn't display website data—it is only there in edit mode to allow a user to a add a new row. The following logic should be modified within two existing methods *numberOfRowsInSection* and *cellForRowAtIndexPath*. In *numberOfRowsInSection* replace the existing code with what is shown in grey.

```
- (NSInteger)tableView:(UITableView *)tableView numberOfRowsInSection:(NSInteger)section {
    // Return the number of rows in the section.
    long rows=[self.sitesData count];
    if (tableView.isEditing)
        rows++;
    return rows;
}
```

In cellForRowAtIndexPath method add the rows in grey below:

```
- (UITableViewCell *)tableView:(UITableView *)tableView cellForRowAtIndexPath:(NSIndexPath *)indexPath {
    static NSString *CellIdentifier = @"Cell";
    UITableViewCell *cell = [tableView dequeueReusableCellWithIdentifier:CellIdentifier];

    if (indexPath.row==[self.sitesData count] && tableView.isEditing) {
        if (cell == nil) {
            cell = [[UITableViewCell alloc] initWithFrame:CGRectZero reuseIdentifier:CellIdentifier];
        }
        cell.textLabel.text = @"ADD";
        cell.detailTextLabel.text = @"";
    }
    else {
        if (cell == nil) {
            cell = [[UITableViewCell alloc] initWithStyle:UITableViewCellStyleSubtitle reuseIdentifier:CellIdentifier];
        }

        // Configure the cell data textLabel and detailTextLabel from data
    within the sites data objects.  Note the objectAtIndex pulls out a NSDictionary object into rowdata
    for the current website we want to display
        NSDictionary *rowdata = [self.sitesData objectAtIndex:indexPath.row];
```

```
        cell.textLabel.text = [rowdata objectForKey:@"name"];
        NSString *astr=[rowdata objectForKey:@"site"];
        cell.detailTextLabel.text =  [NSString stringWithFormat:@"%@",astr];
cell.accessoryType = UITableViewCellAccessoryDetailDisclosureButton;

        //Place duck feet icon on row
        NSString *path = [[NSBundle mainBundle] pathForResource:@"Duck29" ofType:@"png"];
        UIImage *theImage = [UIImage imageWithContentsOfFile:path];
        cell.imageView.image = theImage;
    }
    return cell;
}
```

Run the app again and you should be able to delete and add rows when you tap the "Edit" button in the upper right. Tap "ADD" row to add a new row and the "Done" button to complete editing.

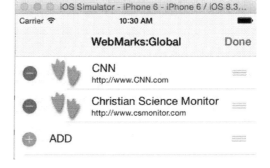

TableView: Cell Selection

One of the most commen actions in a table is to select a row or cell. There are two ways of to implement the selection logic. Usually when tapped, a program should open another screen— for instance, a detail screen for the information in the selected row.

Navigating to a screen from a screen

Note that the following code was already added to the *cellForRowAtIndexPath* routine:

cell.accessoryType = UITableViewCellAccessoryDetailDisclosureButton;

This code will put the information and right arrow icon on the right hand side of a row. If the user taps these icons it means they want to drill into a detail screen for the information in the row.

Add the following method, *accessoryButtonTappedForRowWithIndexPath* , after the current table editing methods. This method will be called when the user taps on the *detail disclosure button* (as the (i) > icon is called) and bring up the view *Detail* that we have already added to our project.

ß

The two lines of code starting "Detail *detailview…" creates a new Detail screen and opens the screen using the *pushViewController*: method. <u>Review these lines of code…they can be used to display any screen from another one when a *navigationController* is used</u>.

```
-(void)tableView:(UITableView *)tableView
accessoryButtonTappedForRowWithIndexPath:(NSIndexPath *)indexPath {
if ([self.sitesData count]) {
    //create Detail screen
    Detail *detailview = [[Detail alloc] initWithNibName:@"Detail" bundle:nil];
  [self.navigationController pushViewController:detailview animated:YES];
  }
}
```

To allow the .m to recognize the new screen, Detail, we must add the following logic at the top of the Sites.m file:

```
#import "Detail.h"
```

When we **run the app** now and tap a detail disclosure button you will notice a blank detail screen appears as shown at the right.

You can return to the WebMarks screen by tapping the "<WebMarks" button at the top left of the Detail screen.

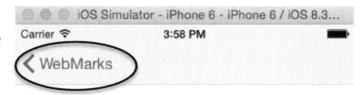

This 'navigate back' functionality is automatically added when we navigate to the Detail screen by the *UINavigationController* object we created for the Sites screen in the *AppDelegate.m* logic when the application opens and creates the TabBar and Sites and Browser screens.

Chapter 5: Creating a Basic View Screen

The following section enables the Detail screen to edit one website's information. It shows how a standard UIView screen and the *XCode Interface Builder* tools work to draw and code a data entry screen with many types of user interface elements such as text boxes, labels, images and switches.

 Click on the *Detail.xib* file in the project view. This brings up the Interface Builder tool that allows you to draw user interface controls onto our UIView named *Detail*.

To size the screen to an iPhone size, click on the right icon (highlighted below with a box around it) and uncheck "Use Auto Layout" then press the button "Disable Size Classes".

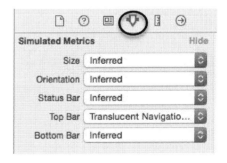 Click on the main view screen in Interface Building and go to its Attributes Inspector by tapping on the icon circled to the right. Set "Top Bar" to "Translucent Navigation Bar". This sets the navigation bar spacing on the screen so that you can start drawing controls under the bar in the visible portion of the screen.

Draw all interface elements as shown below. To add a user interface element, you click on a user interface element in the lower right list of user interface controls and drag it to the view in Interface Builder. You can also copy and paste new user interface elements within the screen by using Command-C and Command-V keyboard commands after selecting a user interface element such as a label.

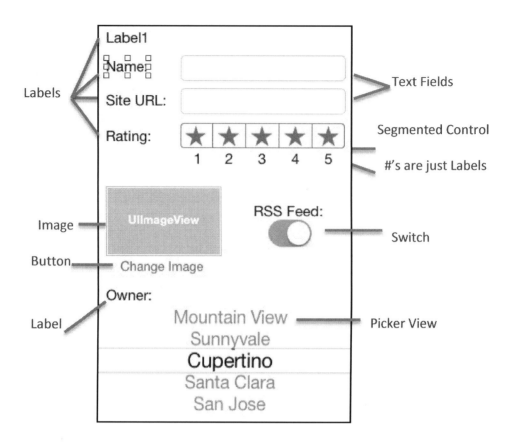

Labels → Label1, Name:, Site URL:, Rating:

Text Fields →

Segmented Control →

#'s are just Labels →

Image → UIImageView

RSS Feed:

Switch →

Button → Change Image

Owner:

Label →

Mountain View
Sunnyvale
Cupertino
Santa Clara
San Jose

Picker View →

To set attributes for controls, click on the 'Attributes Inspector' (circled to the right) then set names of labels, etc. To get the stars in the segment control go to the properties for the segment control and set "Segments" to **5** and for each segment, select the segment (see "Segment" drop-down list to the right), then, set Image to *icon_star.png*.

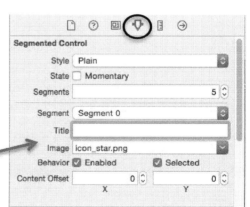

Segmented Control

Style	Plain
State	☐ Momentary
Segments	5
Segment	Segment 0
Title	
Image	icon_star.png
Behavior	☑ Enabled ☑ Selected
Content Offset	0 0
	X Y

The following adds code to support the user interface in the Detail files. Make your Detail.h file look like the following. These are variables that correspond to the various user interface elements we added in the Interface Builder in Step 1.

```objc
#import <UIKit/UIKit.h>
#import "Sites.h"

@interface Detail : UIViewController
{
    BOOL editing;
    int row_id;
    int site_id;
    int site_rank;
    int site_rss;
    int site_group_id;
    NSString *site_name;
    NSString *site_link;
    Sites *atab;

    UIImage *site_image;
    UISwitch *rss_on;
    UIImageView *myimage;
    UISegmentedControl *rating;
    UILabel *label1;
    UITextField *aName;
    UITextField *aSite;
}

@property (nonatomic, retain) Sites *atab;
@property (nonatomic, retain) NSString *site_name;
@property (nonatomic, retain) NSString *site_link;

@property (nonatomic, retain) IBOutlet UIImage *site_image;
@property (nonatomic, retain) IBOutlet UISwitch *rss_on;
@property (nonatomic, retain) IBOutlet UISegmentedControl *rating;
@property (nonatomic, retain) IBOutlet UIImageView *myimage;
@property (nonatomic, retain) IBOutlet UITextField *aName;
@property (nonatomic, retain) IBOutlet UITextField *aSite;
@property (nonatomic, retain) IBOutlet UILabel *label1;

-(IBAction)setEnabled:(id)sender;
-(IBAction)tapButton:(id)sender;

-(void)setValue :(int)site_id :(int)aid :(int)rank :(int)group_id :(NSString *)asite :(NSString *)attr;

@end
```

Variables used by methods in the object are defined here. Int variables only need to be defined once but any object, such as *site_name*, also need a @property as shown in the second instance of (A) above. Note the Sites object and atab variable: we store a reference to our calling screen so that we can call its setValue method to save our data when we are done with the Detail screen.

 All user interface elements that we need to set or get values from get defined as objects here and later again with the *IBOutlet* designator is to identify these properties as user interface accessible properties.

 IBAction identifies user interface accessible methods used by the app's button and switch controls.

 Make your Detail.m file look like the following. These are methods to make the various user interface elements collect data.

```
#import "Detail.h"

@implementation Detail
@synthesize site_link, site_name, site_image, atab, rating;
@synthesize rss_on, myimage, aName, aSite, label1;

-(void)setValue :(int)asite_id :(int)aid :(int)rank :(int)group_id :(NSString *)asite :(NSString *)attr {
    site_link=asite;
    row_id=aid;
    site_id=asite_id;
    site_rank=rank;
    site_group_id=group_id;
    site_image=nil;
    int rssloc=[attr rangeOfString:@"rss"].location;
    site_rss=(rssloc>=0) && (rssloc<1000);
}

- (void)viewDidLoad {
    [super viewDidLoad];

    // Set the initial user interface values to the website information
    [rss_on setOn:(site_rss==1) animated:YES];
    label1.text=[NSString stringWithFormat:@"Site id: %d",site_id];
    label1.font = [UIFont fontWithName:@"Zapfino" size: 10.0];
    aName.text=site_name;
    aSite.text=site_link;
    rating.selectedSegmentIndex=site_rank-1;
    myimage.image=site_image;
}

-(void)viewDidDisappear:(BOOL)animated {
    //When user goes back to Sites screen by pressing < Sites in upper right, system calls
viewDidDisappear and the logic below calls the setValue routine in the Sites object (screen) to
update information for the row designated by row #: row_id. The user modified website name,
URL (aSite.text), site rank and RSS flag attributes are all passed back to the Sites screen.
```

```
    NSString *attr=@"";
    if (site_rss==1)
       attr=@"rss";
    [atab setValue :aName.text :aSite.text :site_rank :site_group_id :row_id :attr];
}
```

```
-(IBAction)setEnabled:(id)sender {
    site_rss=rss_on.isOn;
}

-(IBAction)segmentAction:(id)sender {
    UISegmentedControl *segmentedControl = (UISegmentedControl *)sender;
    site_rank=segmentedControl.selectedSegmentIndex+1;
}

-(IBAction)tapButton:(id)sender {
}
```

@end

An @synthesis statement is needed for each object (not the integers) defined in the .h header file.

The Detail.setValue method sets variables that hold the state of the user interface elements. This method is called by Sites screen when the Detail screen is created to initialize these variables.

viewDidLoad sets all the user interface controls equal to their corresponding variables. The way to set the value of the user interface control varies and is detailed below in the User Interface Elements section.

This setValue method is calling the one in the Sites screen when the Detail screen is closed (when the user navigates back to the Sites screen). This method thus saves the changes we made in the Detail screen.

The setEnabled, segmentAction, tabButton and textFieldShouldReturn methods support taps from users on user interface elements. The logic for each control is detailed below in the User Interface Elements section

Within Sites.m add the following code to ensure that changes in the values in the Detail screen get saved back to our Sites screen data structures:

a) call the Detail screen's *setValue* logic when the Detail screen is first created in the *accessoryButtonTappedForRowWithIndexPath* method (this is the method that is called when tapping the detail disclosure (i)> button on a row), and

b) the code for the Sites *setValue* method which will be called by Detail.m when the user leaves the Detail screen. This *setValue* method saves the user's edited values back to the Sites screen's *sitesData* array—the array where we store all website information we display in the screen.

```
-(void)tableView:(UITableView *)tableView
accessoryButtonTappedForRowWithIndexPath:(NSIndexPath *)indexPath
{
    //This logic gets the current row from the sites array
    NSUInteger row = [indexPath row];
    NSDictionary *rowdata = [self.sitesData objectAtIndex:row];

    if ([self.sitesData count]) {
    //These code lines put the current website row's data into variables
    //that will be passed to the Detail screen.
        int site_id=[[rowdata objectForKey:@"id"] integerValue];
        int rank=[[rowdata objectForKey:@"rank"] integerValue];
        int group_id=[[rowdata objectForKey:@"group_id"] integerValue];
        NSString *name=[rowdata objectForKey:@"name"];
        NSString *attr=[rowdata objectForKey:@"attributes"];

        //create Detail screen
        Detail *detailview = [[Detail alloc] initWithNibName:@"Detail" bundle:nil];
        detailview.site_name=name;
        detailview.atab=self;
        [detailview setValue:site_id :row :rank :group_id :[rowdata objectForKey:@"site"] :attr];
        [self.navigationController pushViewController:detailview animated:YES];
    }
}

-(void)setValue :(NSString *)aname :(NSString *)asite :(int)rank :(int)group_id :(int)arow
:(NSString *)attr {
    //update data in arow object dictionary
    NSDictionary *rowdata = [self.sitesData objectAtIndex:arow];
    int site_id=[[rowdata objectForKey:@"id"] integerValue];
    NSDictionary *row1=[[NSDictionary alloc] initWithObjectsAndKeys:[NSNumber
numberWithInt:site_id],@"id",aname, @"name",[NSNumber numberWithInt:rank], @"rank",
[NSNumber numberWithInt:group_id], @"group_id", asite,@"site", attr, @"attributes",nil];
    [self.sitesData replaceObjectAtIndex:arow withObject:row1];
}
```

The replaceObjectAtIndex method is used to replace the currently edited row (arow) in the sitesData array with the new values coming back from the Detail screen.

To ensure the Sites screen refreshes, add the following method, *viewDidAppear,* after the *viewDidLoad* routine in Sites.m. The tableView *reloadData* method will refresh the entire Table View displayed contents to show the newly edited website information if it has been modified.

```
- (void)viewDidAppear:(BOOL)animated {
```

```
    [self.tableView reloadData];
}
```

 We also need to add the setValue method definition into the Sites.h file so that the Detail screen can access it—make it a *public method.*

```
@property (nonatomic, retain) NSDictionary *default_site;
@property (nonatomic,strong) NSMutableArray  *sites;
-(void)setValue :(NSString *)aname :(NSString *)asite :(int)rank :(int)group_id :(int)arow
:(NSString *)attr;
```

User Interface Elements

We will now look at how to hook the user interface we drew to the code we added—the two must be connected. To hook up the methods and variables to the screen user interface elements we have drawn on to it, click on the Details.xib screen and bring up the User Interface Builder again.

9 The first connection is the view itself must be connected. Right-click on the main view border within interface builder and then drag drop from the circle next to New Referencing Outlet to the yellow box (File's Owner). Select the "view" option that will appear and the properites box should appear as it does to the right. This connects the view to the Detail files.

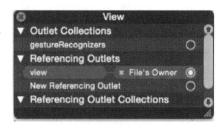

Labels

10 We will use Label1 to display the id of the website record so we will need to change Label1's text in code while the app is running. To do this we need to associate the label with a property (data variable) we can access in our code.

To do this, right-click on the UILabel, *Label1,* control within Interface Builder and a dialog in black appears as shown to the right.

You need to click on the circle next to *Referencing Outlets – New Referencing Outlet* and drag-n-drop to the yellow cube (also shown). A blue line appears. Upon drop, select the option "Label1" as shown to the right.

This operation connects the UILabel object created

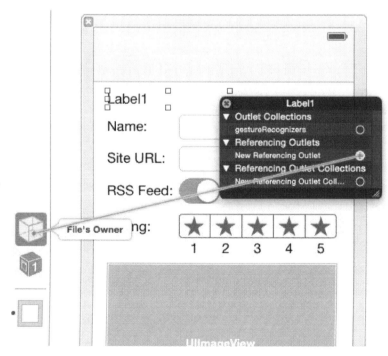

in the Detail.h code with the interface so the code can manipulate it. No other label needs a label property associated with it since no other label needs its text changed in code.

As an example of what we can do with labels see the code method *viewDidLoad* in Detail.m. Note the following code is used to set a labels' text value and its font type and text size. The font and size could have been set in the Interface Builder properties screen for Label1 but all the user interface control properties can also be set in code (as shown here).

```
label1.text = [NSString stringWithFormat:@"Site id: %d",site_id];
label1.font = [UIFont fontWithName:@"Zapfino" size: 10.0];
```

Buttons

To associate the button you created labeled "Change Picture" with the code method "tapButton", click and drag from the circle next to the *Touch up Inside* event to the yellow cube (File's Owner) and select method: *tapButton*. This means that when the user taps the button the *tapButton* method in Detail.m is executed.

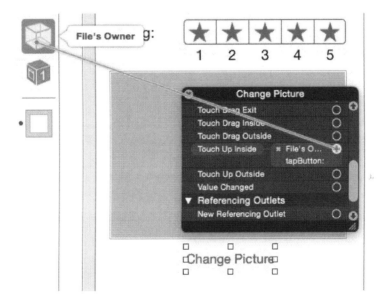

The code for this type of method has the following header format. Any code can be placed within the method to respond to the button tap. Note the IBAction type, however, no return statement is required in this method.

```
-(IBAction)tapButton:(id)sender {

}
```

Text Boxes

A text box has type UITextField. Associate the Site URL text box to the Detail code's property *aSite* by drag-n-dropping from "New Referencing Outlet" to the yellow cube and select "aSite" property. Also drag from the circle next to the *delegate* property in the Outlets area in the black box, to the view (yellow cube). Repeat this procedure for the Name text box but select "aName" property.

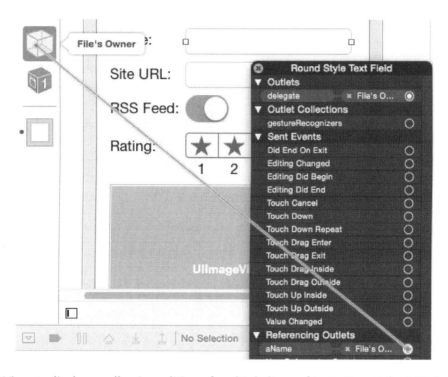

Use a UITextView to display or allowing editing of multiple lines of text. To set the initial value of a text box, see example below from the *viewDidLoad* method of the Detail.m screen:

```
aName.text=site_name;
aSite.text=site_link;
```

You can retrieve any edited value in a similar way. From the *viewDidDisappear* method note the use of <u>aName.text</u> again to pass the text value to the *setValue* method in the Sites screen:

```
[atab setValue :aName.text :aSite.text :site_rank :row_id :attr];
```

One can also assign this to a variable such as in the code:
```
NSString *astr=aName.text;
```

Getting the keyboard to go away

When editing text fields you need to add a method such as the following to make the keyboard go away from the screen when the user is done typing.

13   Within the Detail.h screen add <UITextFieldDelegate> as follows:

```
@interface Detail : UIViewController <UITextFieldDelegate>
```

And add the following method to the Detail.m code:

```
- (BOOL)textFieldShouldReturn:(UITextField *)textField
{
    [aName resignFirstResponder];
    return YES;
}
```

Switchs

A switch allows a Boolean value to be set.

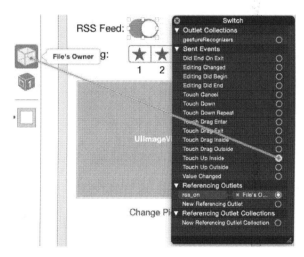

14   Right-click on the green switch control and set the "New Referencing Outlet" property to the **"rss_on"** property by dragging from the circle to the view (yellow box). Also set "Touch up inside" to the method ***setEnabled***. So when the user toggles the switch by tapping on it the code in the setEnabled button will access the current value and save it in the Detail view's property.

```
-(IBAction)setEnabled:(id)sender {
    site_rss=rss_on.isOn;
}
```

In the viewDidLoad method we set the switch's value when the screen opens. Note (site_rss==1) returns a Boolean value.

```
[rss_on setOn:(site_rss==1) animated:YES];
```

Segmented Controls

Segment controls allow the user to choose from a set of items (a multi-choice box). Through the properties you can add one or more segments to the segment control and the segments are usually identified by adding a short piece of text or an image to each segment using the properties screen within Interface Builder.

 As before, set the "New referencing Outlet" in the black box for the segmented control to "**rating**" property. This allows us to set and access the value of the segment control. Also associate "**Value Changed**" event with the Detail method: **segmentAction**. When the user taps the segment we store the value of the segment into the variable site_rank. Note we add 1 to the rank because the value returned is zero-based and we want rank to be a value from 1 to 5.

```
-(IBAction)segmentAction:(id)sender {
    UISegmentedControl *segmentedControl = (UISegmentedControl *)sender;
    site_rank=segmentedControl.selectedSegmentIndex+1;
}
```

Code to access the segment looks like the following from Detail:

```
rating.selectedSegmentIndex=site_rank-1;
```

UIPickerView

These controls allow the user to select from a list of known values or select a date (using the UIDatePicker).

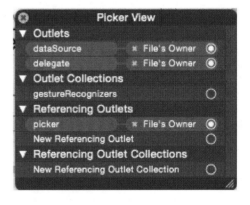

 To set the UIPickerView we added to the screen, make the code changes below to add picker logic to the Detail.h and Detail.m files then set the properties as per the image to the right (File's Owner is the yellow cube for the screen). Be sure to set the code first before setting the Interface Builder properties as the properties must be defined in code before they can be referenced.

Replace Detail.h interface line with:

```
@interface Detail : UIViewController <UITextFieldDelegate, UIPickerViewDataSource,
UIPickerViewDelegate>
```

Add to Detail.h:

```
NSArray *_pickerdata;
```

```
@property (weak, nonatomic) IBOutlet UIPickerView *picker;
@property (nonatomic, retain) NSArray *_pickerdata;
```

All objects defined in Detail.h must be included in a *@synthesize* statement. Place at top of Detail.m after "@implmentation Detail" line:

```
@synthesize _pickerdata, picker;
```

Place as last line in *viewDidLoad*: method in Detail.m:

```
_pickerdata = @[@"Everyone", @"Myself", @"Group A", @"Group B", @"Group C", @"Group D"];
```

Add this method to set the selected value of the picker when the screen opens:

```
-(void)viewDidAppear:(BOOL)animated {
   [picker selectRow:site_group_id inComponent:0 animated:YES];
}
```

Place the routines below to initialize values in the picker. These routines should be placed after *textFieldShouldReturn* method in Detail.m:

```
// The number of columns of data
- (int)numberOfComponentsInPickerView:(UIPickerView *)pickerView
{
   return 1;
}

// The number of rows of data
- (int)pickerView:(UIPickerView *)pickerView numberOfRowsInComponent:(NSInteger)component
{
   return _pickerdata.count;
}

// The data to return for the row and component (column) that's being passed in
- (NSString*)pickerView:(UIPickerView *)pickerView titleForRow:(NSInteger)row
forComponent:(NSInteger)component
{
   return _pickerdata[row];
}

// Catpure the picker view selection
- (void)pickerView:(UIPickerView *)pickerView didSelectRow:(NSInteger)row
inComponent:(NSInteger)component
{
   // This method is triggered whenever the user makes a change to the picker selection.
   // The parameter named row and component represents what was selected.
   site_group_id=row;
}
```

Images and Camera Access

To use images we hook up the image control is a similar way as other controls. Associate the "New referencing Outlet" to the property *myimage*.

Image control images can be set directly in the Interface Builder properties screen for the control or from code. Following is the sample code from Sites.m that sets an image icon for each row of the TableView:

```
NSString *path = [[NSBundle mainBundle] pathForResource:@"Duck29" ofType:@"png"];
UIImage *theImage = [UIImage imageWithContentsOfFile:path];
cell.imageView.image = theImage;
```

Note that the path string pulls images from the application project. Code such as the following would pull the image from the applications documents folder (note every app is assigned a documents folder on the device it is running).

```
NSArray *paths = NSSearchPathForDirectoriesInDomains(NSDocumentDirectory,
NSUserDomainMask, YES);
    NSString *documentsDirectory=[[paths objectAtIndex:0]
stringByAppendingPathComponent:@"Duck29.png"];
        UIImage *theImage = [UIImage imageWithContentsOfFile: documentsDirectory];
        cell.imageView.image = theImage;
```

18 The following code should be added to the **tapButton** method of Detail.m to allow the camera and camera roll to provide an image for the image in the Detail screen. The *imagePickerController* is used to do this. Note that the tapButton method was added previously for the button control.

```
-(IBAction)tapButton:(id)sender {
    UIImagePickerController *imagePicker = [[UIImagePickerController alloc] init];

    // If the device ahs a camera, take a picture, otherwise,
    // just pick from the photo library
    if ([UIImagePickerController
isSourceTypeAvailable:UIImagePickerControllerSourceTypeCamera]) {
        imagePicker.sourceType = UIImagePickerControllerSourceTypeCamera;
    } else {
        imagePicker.sourceType = UIImagePickerControllerSourceTypePhotoLibrary;
    }

    imagePicker.delegate = self;

    // Place image picker on the screen
    [self presentViewController:imagePicker animated:YES completion:NULL];
}
```

A
```
- (void)imagePickerController:(UIImagePickerController *)picker
didFinishPickingMediaWithInfo:(NSDictionary *)info
{
    // Get picked image from info dictionary
    UIImage *image = info[UIImagePickerControllerOriginalImage];
```

```
// Put that image onto the screen in our image view
self.myimage.image = image;

// Take image picker off the screen -
// you must call this dismiss method
[self dismissViewControllerAnimated:YES completion:NULL];
}
```

 The method *imagePickerController* is called when the user has finished either picking a picture from camera roll or taking a new picture. The following line of code below actually assigns the image from the Picker to the image on the screen:

```
self.myimage.image = image;
```

Sliders and Steppers

There are no sliders or steppers in the sample app but the following description is provided for them.

The slider or stepper allows the user to set a numeric value using a slide control or a +/- single value 'stepper' control. From the properties screen for the UISlider or UIStepper you can set a min, max and default value for the control. You can associate methods and properties as before with these controls by using the "New referencing Outlet" Referencing Outlet and the "Touch up inside" event. An example setSlider method might be the following (which also shows how to reference slider values). Note steppers and sliders both use the value property to get the current value.

```
-(IBAction) setSlider:(id)sender {
    sliderValue=mySlider.value];
}
```

Run and the Detail view should be able to be brought up for editing of a website. Note: you may need the Testing methods in the following chapter if one of the previous steps didn't work. Also, check all properties in the Interface Builder and ensure all the controls are hooked up.

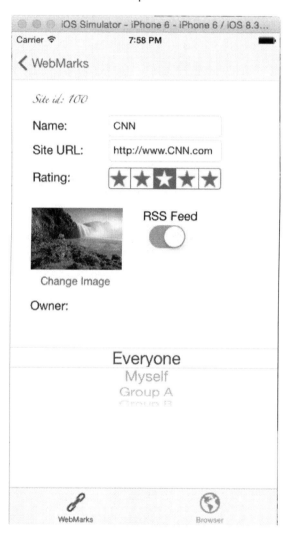

Standard view methods

There are several standard methods that get called whenever a screen is navigated to, opened, navigated away from, or removed from memory (closed). These methods are often commented out in a new view .m file and you can just uncomment them and use them or you may have to re-type the header. To retype the header just type "–(void)view" and prototype headers will appear from which you can select the method you wish. The methods are:

viewDidLoad   called after the graphics are displayed but only once upon loading
viewWillAppear   gets called before viewDidLoad, before graphic images are displayed.
viewDidAppear   gets called after the initial display. This is the last chance to initialize
                               anything before control gets passed to the user.
viewWillDisappear Before the view is navigated away from
viewDidDisappear Just after the view is navigated away from
viewDidUnload   After the view is removed from memory but before control is returned.

Chapter 6: Testing

There are three testing and debugging techniques described below: logging, tracing and alert messages. Each approach has its place to help get your code working. In general, your app should be run in the simulator for both iPhone and iPad (if supported in app) and then tested on an actual device. To test on a device plug the device into your computer with the USB cable and follow the instructions that will appear to set up the device as a development and testing device.

Debugging: Trace

Tracing is a built-in feature of XCode and involves setting breakpoints in the code and then stepping through the code one line at a time. Follow the instructions below to see how it works:

1. Set breakpoints before sections of code you want to step through. Set trace breakpoints in code by tapping in the column to left of code and a > mark appears as shown below.
2. Click Run button in the upper left to run the program as usual. When the program gets to the point in the program where you set the breakpoint it will stop and highlight the breakpoint in the code.
3. At this point, use the step and run trace buttons (circled below) to step through the code. You can 'float' over variables to see their current values while tracing or look at the bottom screen below the code to see the variables that are in scope and their values. The picture below shows a breakpoint and variables.

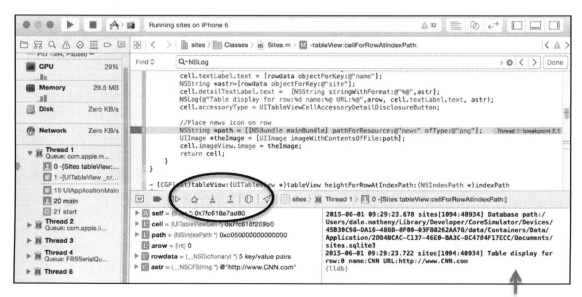

Log Output Window

48

As an example trace put a breakmark in sites.m cellForRowAtIndexPath metod on the line starting "NSString *path..." and run the app. It will stop for each row displayed in the Sites screen.

Debugging: Logs

The log statement can be used as shown below to trace through code by leaving 'bread crumbs'. Each log statement will leave a message in the message log window in the lower right below the code (shown in the window above). It is handy because it doesn't interfere with the flow of the program. Be sure to include logging statements at critical points and the results of the log appear in the output window at the bottom of the code window. See above.

Code is required for each log statement. The example below shows how the NSLog statement works. It takes a string with formatting commands for inserting variable values. Note %@ is for string variables and %d for integer values.

The code below should be inserted in *cellForRowAtIndexPath* method in Sites.m.

```
cell.detailTextLabel.text = [NSString stringWithFormat:@"%@",astr];
NSLog(@"Table display for row:%d name:%@",indexPath.row, cell.textLabel.text);
cell.accessoryType = UITableViewCellAccessoryDetailDisclosureButton;
```

The messages will appear in a bottom log window within the development environment during runtime.

Debugging: Alerts

An alert actually shows an error message to the user and they must OK to proceed. See the example below that is added to the Detail screen when the user presses the RSS switch to ON.

Add the following code to the Detail.m setEnabled method and re-run to see the alert as pictured.

```
-(IBAction)setEnabled:(id)sender {
    site_rss=rss_on.isOn;

 if (site_rss==1) {
    UIAlertController * alert= [UIAlertController
                    alertControllerWithTitle:@"Switch"
                    message:@"You set the RSS switch on.  Assumption is that this website
is an RSS feed."
                    preferredStyle:UIAlertControllerStyleAlert];
    UIAlertAction* ok = [UIAlertAction
                actionWithTitle:@"OK"
```

```
                    style:UIAlertActionStyleDefault
                    handler:^(UIAlertAction * action)
                    {
                      [alert dismissViewControllerAnimated:YES completion:nil];
                    }];
        [alert addAction:ok]; // add action to uialertcontroller
        [self presentViewController:alert animated:YES completion:nil];
    }
}
```

Chapter 7: Web Browsing

The Browser screen is implemented using the object
"viewer". The viewer.h, .m and .xib files are pre-developed
to contain a UIWebView which is a browser control
provided by Apple. You may easily re-use viewer.h, .m and
.xib anytime you need a rudimentary browser screen—just
copy the files into your project. Note that these browsers
can also also display .pdf files. Review the code in
viewer.m to see how the UIWebView works. Viewer also
has routines that allow forward and backward web page
movement.

The Browser screen is initialized to go to the Google
website in AppDeletate.m when it is created. This is
accomplished with this line of code:

```
viewController2.Url=[NSURL
URLWithString:@"http://www.google.com"];
```

When the user clicks on the browser icon in the TabBar the
user is presented with the screen to the right. Later in this
book we will add functionality to bookmark the current
web page by inserting a website into our website data.

Display Website

A key piece of functionality is to actually display the website that we are saving in our Sites
application. With our generic viewer object web browser we can do this quite easily when the
user taps on a website within the Sites screen.

Add the following code to implement the website browser called from the Sites
screen. Add the viewer header file import statement to the top of Sites.m:
```
#import "Sites.h"
#import "Detail.h"
#import "viewer.h"
```

Add the following method after the setValue method in Sites.m to create a browser screen
when the user taps websites in the Sites screen.

```
- (void)tableView:(UITableView *)tableView didSelectRowAtIndexPath:(NSIndexPath *)indexPath
{
    NSDictionary *rowdata = [self.sitesData objectAtIndex:indexPath.row];
    viewer *controller = [[viewer alloc] initWithNibName:@"viewer" bundle:nil];
```

```
controller.Url=[NSURL URLWithString:[rowdata objectForKey:@"site"]];
[controller setViewType:0];
controller.navigationItem.title=@"Browser";
[self.navigationController pushViewController:controller animated:YES];
}
```

Run the program and the browser work by tapping the CS Monitor row.

Chapter 8: Using a Local Database for App Data Storage

WebMarks is working except one key factor: when you come back into the app all the default data is back—you can't save, *persist*, data. In this section we create a SQLite database which is a common database used for local data storage for apps. It will not allow for shared data but is great for local data storage for an app.

Database and SQL Summary

Databases use SQL (Structured Query Language) to manipulate data and store data in tables with rows of data—much like a spreadsheet but with more capacity and flexibility. The four main statements in the SQL language are:

Create   Creates a table in the database.

Select   Queries one or more database tables for data. Can include 'where' criteria to narrow the query results and an 'order' statement to sort the results.

Insert   Inserts one (or more) rows of data into the database.

Delete   Deletes one (or more) rows of data from the database. Can include the 'where' criteria.

Adding libraries

Many libraries of code are provided by iOS to support device functions. Before using a database you must add the SQLITE code library named "libsqlite3.0.dylib" to the project.

Click on "WebMarks" application at the top of the project window. Click on the right on the "Build Phases" tab and open "Link Binary with Libraries". Click the +

(add) button and you will see the dialog to the right. Search using the term "sql" and then click on *libsqlite3.0.dylib*. Press the "Add" button. Also add library "libxml2.dylib" to support our XML parsing in Chapter 9. Your final screen should appear as:

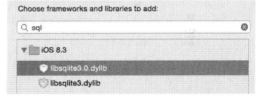

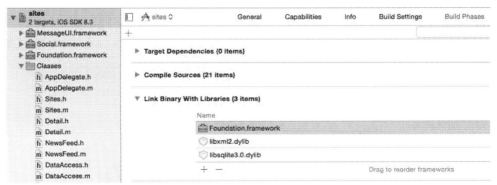

Creating a database

First, we create a new file to store all of our data access routines—this is a key architectural concept, to separate the data from the interface code. This allows us to modify data access separately from the interface. Within this file we will create extract (select), delete and insert/update methods that will support these actions in our Sites screen to save the data permanently.

Create the **DataAccess** object as by going to the File menu, New/File selection. The following screen opens and you should select "Cocoa Touch Class" and press **Next**. In the next screen type select subclass of NSObject and Class name "DataAccess. Press **Next** and **Create**.

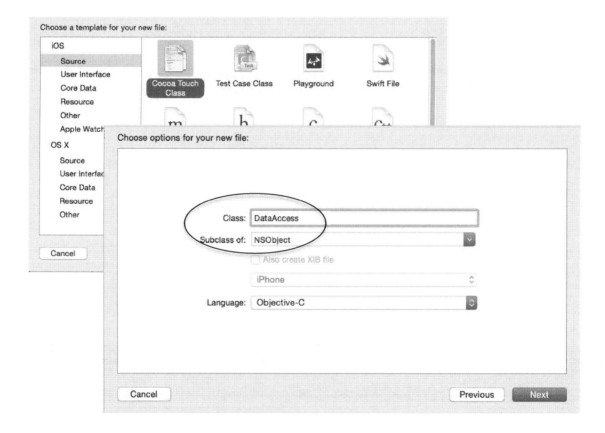

Next we set the DataAccess.h header definition for accessing the database and the four data access routines we will be creating. Copy and paste the following to the header.

A

```
#import <UIKit/UIKit.h>

//Add these imports
#import "sqlite3.h"
#define kFilename @"sites.sqlite3"
#define kDataType 2  //1=NSMutableData array/dictionary only   2=SQLite database
3=MYSQL Database on server (shared data)
```

B

```
@interface DataAccess : NSObject {
    sqlite3 *database;
}

-(void) checkDB;
-(void) sitesLoad :(NSMutableArray *)linksarray :(int)group_id :(id)obj;
-(void) sitesDelete :(int)site_id :(id)obj;
-(int)sitesInsertUpdate:(NSString *)name :(NSString *)site :(int)site_id :(int)rank :(int)group_id
:(NSString *)attr :(id)obj;
@end
```

A   The import of sqlite3.h enables database functionality in the object.

B   The *database* object variable is of type "sqlite3".

We will now add the method *checkDB* to create a database on each device the app runs by checking each time the app opens to see if the database exists and if it doesn't then it will create it. The first time the app runs the database won't exist and the *checkDB* method will create the database.

4   The following method should be copied into the DataAccess.m file and provides creation of the *sites.sqlite3* database. One table, Links, is created. **Study the following SQL code and the comments (in the code and after the code) and you'll understand how to work with databases using the Select, Insert and Create statements.**

```
- (NSString *)dataFilePath {
    NSArray *paths = NSSearchPathForDirectoriesInDomains(NSDocumentDirectory,
NSUserDomainMask, YES);
    NSString *documentsDirectory = [paths objectAtIndex:0];
    return [documentsDirectory stringByAppendingPathComponent:kFilename];
}

-(void) checkDB {
    NSLog(@"Database path:%@",[self dataFilePath]);

    //open the database
    if (sqlite3_open([[self dataFilePath] UTF8String], &database) != SQLITE_OK) {
        sqlite3_close(database);
        NSLog(@"Failed to open database");
    }
```

```objc
//Create a SQL string with a SQL query to create the database
char *errorMsg;
NSString *createSQL = @"CREATE TABLE IF NOT EXISTS Links (id INTEGER, name TEXT,
link TEXT, rank INTEGER, attributes TEXT, group_id INTEGER);";

//Execute a SQL command to create the table Links
if (sqlite3_exec (database, [createSQL  UTF8String],NULL, NULL, &errorMsg) != SQLITE_OK)
{
    sqlite3_close(database);
    NSLog(@"Error creating table: %s", errorMsg);
}

//Create a sql stmt
sqlite3_stmt *stmt;
//prepare our select (query) SQL to get a count of records in the Links table.
int rec_count=0;
NSString *query =@"SELECT count(*) FROM Links";
//Prepare and execute the query.  The sqlite3_step function gets the first record
if (sqlite3_prepare_v2( database, [query UTF8String],-1, &stmt, nil) == SQLITE_OK) {
    if (sqlite3_step(stmt) == SQLITE_ROW) {
        //use this statement to retreive the 0th (1st) element in the row from the query: the count
of records
        rec_count = sqlite3_column_int(stmt, 0);
    }
}
//finish query execution
sqlite3_finalize(stmt);

//if there are no records insert 3 default records into our database.
if (rec_count==0) {
    int site_id=1;
    NSString *astr=@"http://www.CNN.com";
    NSString *insert  = @"INSERT INTO Links (id, name, link, rank, attributes, group_id) values
(?,'CNN',?,3,'',0);";
    if (sqlite3_prepare_v2(database, [insert UTF8String], -1, &stmt, nil) == SQLITE_OK) {
        //when we use ? in the query we need to 'bind' data to the ? parameters using the
following functions.  Note there are int and text versions of the bind command.
        sqlite3_bind_int(stmt, 1, site_id);
        sqlite3_bind_text(stmt, 2, [astr UTF8String], -1, NULL);
    }
    //execute the insert statement.
    if (sqlite3_step(stmt) != SQLITE_DONE) NSLog(@"Error updating table");
    sqlite3_finalize(stmt);

    site_id=2;
    astr=@"http://www.csmonitor.com";
    insert = @"INSERT INTO Links (id, name, link, rank, attributes, group_id) values
(?,'Christian Science Monitor',?,4,'',0);";
    if (sqlite3_prepare_v2(database, [insert UTF8String], -1, &stmt, nil) == SQLITE_OK) {
        sqlite3_bind_int(stmt, 1, site_id);
        sqlite3_bind_text(stmt, 2, [astr UTF8String], -1, NULL);
    }
    if (sqlite3_step(stmt) != SQLITE_DONE) NSLog(@"Error updating table");
```

```
    sqlite3_finalize(stmt);

    insert  = @"INSERT INTO Links (id, name, link, rank, attributes, group_id) values (3,'CNN
Top Stories','http://rss.cnn.com/rss/cnn_topstories.rss',0,'rss',0)";
    if (sqlite3_prepare_v2(database, [insert UTF8String], -1, &stmt, nil) == SQLITE_OK) {}
    if (sqlite3_step(stmt) != SQLITE_DONE) NSLog(@"Error updating table");
    sqlite3_finalize(stmt);


  }

  //finally, close the database.
  sqlite3_close(database);
}
```

sqlite3_open statement opens the database. *dataFilePath* method gives the path and name of the database to be opened. The *sqlite3_exec* method executes the SQL database create statement stored in the *createSQL* string.

The example below outlines the code needed to perform a SQL select, insert, or delete statement:

```
if (sqlite3_open([[self dataFilePath] UTF8String], &database) != SQLITE_OK) {
    sqlite3_close(database);
    NSLog(@"Failed to open database");
}

sqlite3_stmt *stmt;
NSString *query =@"SELECT id, name FROM Links where owner=?";

if (sqlite3_prepare_v2(database, [query UTF8String], -1, &stmt, nil) == SQLITE_OK) {
    sqlite3_bind_int(stmt, 1, owner);
}

while (sqlite3_step(statement) == SQLITE_ROW) {
    link_id=sqlite3_column_int(statement,0);
    char *namec = (char *)sqlite3_column_text(statement, 1);
    if (namec==nil) namec="";
    NSString *name = [NSString stringWithUTF8String:namec];
}

sqlite3_finalize(stmt);
sqlite3_close(database);
```

In this select query statement the *sqlite3_prepare_v2* method is used to prepare the query. Parameters are passed using the bind methods: *sqlite3_bind_int* and *sqlite3_bind_text* which insert data into the corresponding '?' symbols in the SQL that was prepared for execution. Note the 1 in the first bind corresponds to the first '?', the 2nd bind uses '2' to match the second '?', if it exists, etc.

The *sqlite3_step* function executes the query and then loops for each query result row. *sqlite3_column_int*(stmt, 0) and *sqlite3_column_text*(stmt, 1) methods can be used to retrieve data from the records passed back as the result of the query where the '0' or '1' parameter is the zero-based index to the field being returned. Note the use of the char datatype: all text fields are returned as C-language char fields and the 3 lines of code above shows how to convert them to a NSString string object while also checking for null (empty) string values. Every *sqlite3_prepare* statement must have a *sqlite3_finalize* to finalize the query.

 The final database statement is the *sqlite3_close(database)* statement.

 Finally, we hook up a call to the checkDB method from the AppDelegate.m routine that gets called each time the application opens.

```
#import "AppDelegate.h"
#import "Sites.h"
#import "viewer.h"
#import "DataAccess.h"
```

Add to *didFinishLaunchingWithOptions* method toward the bottom:

```
//Initialize the database
DataAccess *aData = [[DataAccess alloc] init];
[aData checkDB];
self.window.backgroundColor = [UIColor whiteColor];
[self.window makeKeyAndVisible];
```

Database access for debugging

It is often useful to access the data in the database directly for debugging purposes or to formulate correct SQL queries. To do so, note the output of the NSLog statement in the output window below that was put into the *dataFilePath* method—a method that formulates the

```
        //Place news icon on row
        NSString *path = [[NSBundle mainBundle] pathForResource:@"news" ofType:@"png"];    Thread 1: breakpoint 2.1
        UIImage *theImage = [UIImage imageWithContentsOfFile:path];
        cell.imageView.image = theImage;
        return cell;
    }
}

- (CGFloat)tableView:(UITableView *)tableView heightForRowAtIndexPath:(NSIndexPath *)indexPath
```

```
▶ A  self = (Sites ") 0x7fc618e7ad80
▶ L  cell = (UITableViewCell ") 0x7fc618f269b0
▶ L  path = (NSIndexPath ") 0xc050000000000000
   L  arow = (int) 0
▶ L  rowdata = (__NSDictionary!") 5 key/value pairs
▶ L  astr = (__NSCFString ") @"http://www.CNN.com"
```

```
2015-06-01 09:29:23.678 sites[1094:40934] Database path:/
Users/dale.matheny/Library/Developer/CoreSimulator/Devices/
45B38C98-DA16-4B8B-8F00-03FB0262AA76/data/Containers/Data/
Application/2D84BCAC-C137-46E0-BA3C-BC4784F17ECC/Documents/
sites.sqlite3
2015-06-01 09:29:23.722 sites[1094:40934] Table display for
row:0 name:CNN URL:http://www.CNN.com
(lldb)
```

database path name. This is the database path—the location of the simulator database. You can copy and enter this path with the name of the database into a SQL tool such as Navicat for SQLite (sold by Navicat, Inc.). With a tool such as Navicat for SQLite you can see the active records in tables, create tables and databases or add/remove table columns and run SQL directly on the database. A free version of Navicat for SQLite can be found at the link: *http://www.navicat.com/download*

The image below shows the Navicat for SQLite tool open to the current contents of the Links table:

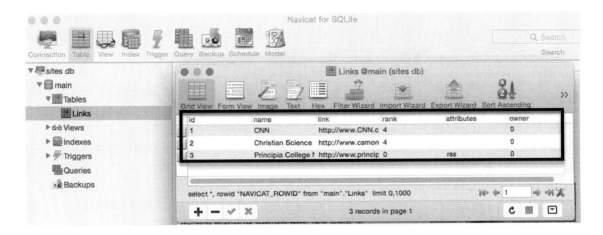

Database: Querying records and extracting data

6 Insert the following methods in DataAccess.m to allow the app to select all website records from Links. This will be hooked up to the Load of the Sites screen to initialize all website data stored currently. The code below selects all data from the database and creates a mutable data array to store the data.

```objc
-(void)sitesLoad:(NSMutableArray *)linksarray :(int)group_id :(id)obj{
    [self sitesDBLoad:linksarray :group_id];
}

-(void)sitesDBLoad :(NSMutableArray *)linksarray :(int)group_id {
    if (sqlite3_open([[self dataFilePath] UTF8String], &database) != SQLITE_OK) {
        sqlite3_close(database);
        NSAssert(0, @"Failed to open database");
    }

    NSString *select = [NSString stringWithFormat:@"SELECT id,name,link,rank,attributes from
Links where group_id=%d;",group_id];
    sqlite3_stmt *statement;
    int link_id, rank;
    if (sqlite3_prepare_v2( database, [select UTF8String],-1, &statement, nil) == SQLITE_OK) {
        while (sqlite3_step(statement) == SQLITE_ROW) {
            link_id=sqlite3_column_int(statement,0);
            rank=sqlite3_column_int(statement,3);

            char *namec = (char *)sqlite3_column_text(statement, 1);
            if (namec==nil) namec="";
            NSString *name = [NSString stringWithUTF8String:namec];

            char *linkc = (char *)sqlite3_column_text(statement, 2);
            if (linkc==nil) linkc="";
            NSString *link = [NSString stringWithUTF8String:linkc];

            char *attrc = (char *)sqlite3_column_text(statement,4);
            if (attrc==nil) attrc="";
            NSString *attr = [NSString stringWithUTF8String:attrc];

            NSDictionary *row1=[[NSDictionary alloc] initWithObjectsAndKeys:[NSNumber
numberWithInt:link_id], @"id", name, @"name", link, @"site",[NSNumber
numberWithInt:rank],@"rank", attr, @"attributes", nil];
            [linksarray addObject:row1];
        }
        sqlite3_finalize(statement);
    }

    sqlite3_close(database);
}
```

Add the following to Sites.m file in the appropriate places to support calling the new DataAccess object and related database methods.

```
#import "DataAccess.h"
@implementation Sites
DataAccess * aData;
```

 Modify the sites.m *viewDidLoad* and *viewDidAppear* methods to comment out the *manualLoad* method and load data into the *sitesData* array from the SQLite database when the screen is first loaded into memory.

```
- (void)viewDidLoad {
    [super viewDidLoad];
    aData = [[DataAccess alloc] init];

    default_site=[[NSDictionary alloc] initWithObjectsAndKeys:[NSNumber
numberWithInt:0],@"id",@"", @"name",@"",@"site",[NSNumber
numberWithInt:0],@"rank",@"",@"attributes",nil];
    //[self manualLoad];   // Local Objection C++ data structures -- non-persistent

    // Uncomment the following line to preserve selection between presentations.
    // self.clearsSelectionOnViewWillAppear = NO;

    // Uncomment the following line to display an Edit button in the navigation bar for this view
controller.
    self.navigationItem.rightBarButtonItem = self.editButtonItem;
}

- (void)viewDidAppear:(BOOL)animated {
    if (sitesData==nil)
        self.sitesData = [NSMutableArray new];
    else {
        [self.sitesData removeAllObjects];
    }
    [aData sitesLoad:self.sitesData :0 :self]; //group=0 default group
    [self.tableView reloadData];
}
```

Run the app and you should see the three default records created in CheckDB appear in the Sites screen. Now we can move on to enabling the delete and insert/update editing database support to complete the SQLite database implementation so that you can save all changes when you re-open the app.

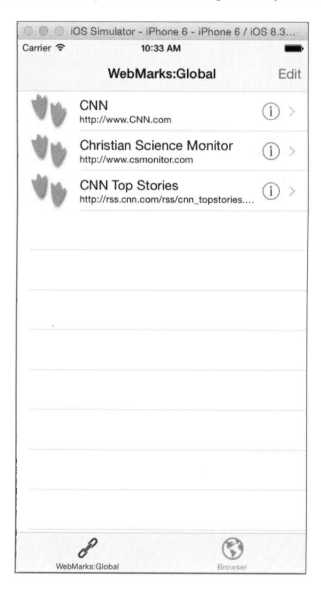

Database: Deleting records

 Insert the following method in DataAccess.m to allow the app to delete a record from Links. This will be hooked up to the delete function of the Sites screen to remove a website when the user deletes one through the UITableView editing logic.

```
-(void)sitesDBDelete :(int)site_id {
  if (sqlite3_open([[self dataFilePath] UTF8String], &database) != SQLITE_OK) {
    sqlite3_close(database);
    NSLog(@"Failed to open database deleteRecord");
  }

  sqlite3_stmt *stmt;
  char *update = "DELETE FROM links WHERE id=?;";
  if (sqlite3_prepare_v2(database, update, -1, &stmt, nil) == SQLITE_OK) {
    sqlite3_bind_int(stmt, 1, site_id);
  }
  if (sqlite3_step(stmt) != SQLITE_DONE)
    NSLog(@"Error delete patients treatments");
  sqlite3_finalize(stmt);

  sqlite3_close(database);
}

-(void)sitesDelete :(int)site_id :(id)obj {
  [self sitesDBDelete:site_id];
}
```

The call to *sitesDelete* needs to be added to the *commitEditingStyle* method within Sites.m to delete a site when the user does this in the Sites screen. Logic exists to delete from the *sitesData* data structure and the *tableView* but no it must also be deleted from the data store.

```
- (void)tableView:(UITableView *)tableView
commitEditingStyle:(UITableViewCellEditingStyle)editingStyle forRowAtIndexPath:(NSIndexPath
*)indexPath {
  if (editingStyle == UITableViewCellEditingStyleDelete)
  {
    NSDictionary *rowdata = [sitesData objectAtIndex:indexPath.row];
    int site_id=[[rowdata objectForKey:@"id"] intValue];
    [aData sitesDelete:site_id :self];
    [self.sitesData removeObjectAtIndex:indexPath.row];
    [tableView deleteRowsAtIndexPaths:@[indexPath]
withRowAnimation:UITableViewRowAnimationFade];
```

Database: Inserting and Updating records

Insert the following method in DataAccess.m to allow the app to insert or update a website record within the database Links table. This will be hooked up to the update function called when the user finishes editing within the Detail screen.

```
-(int)sitesDBInsertUpdate:(NSString *)name :(NSString *)site :(int)site_id :(int)rank :(int)group_id
:(NSString *)attr
{
  if (sqlite3_open([[self dataFilePath] UTF8String], &database) != SQLITE_OK) {
    sqlite3_close(database);
    NSLog(@"Failed to open database savedetail");
  }

  char *errorMsg;
  char *update = "begin;";
  if (sqlite3_exec (database,update,NULL, NULL, &errorMsg) != SQLITE_OK) {NSLog(@"Error
begin %s", errorMsg);}

  sqlite3_stmt *stmt;
  if (site_id==0) { //insert new row
    NSString *query =@"SELECT count(*) FROM Links";
    if (sqlite3_prepare_v2( database, [query UTF8String],-1, &stmt, nil) == SQLITE_OK) {
      if (sqlite3_step(stmt) == SQLITE_ROW) {
        site_id = sqlite3_column_int(stmt, 0)+1;
      }
    }
    sqlite3_finalize(stmt);

    update = "INSERT INTO Links (id, name, link, rank, group_id, attributes) VALUES (?, ?, ?, ?,
?, ?);";
    if (sqlite3_prepare_v2(database, update, -1, &stmt, nil) == SQLITE_OK) {
      sqlite3_bind_int(stmt, 1, site_id);
      sqlite3_bind_text(stmt, 2, [[NSString stringWithFormat:@"%@", name] UTF8String], -1,
NULL);
      sqlite3_bind_text(stmt, 3, [[NSString stringWithFormat:@"%@", site] UTF8String], -1,
NULL);
      sqlite3_bind_int(stmt, 4, rank);
      sqlite3_bind_int(stmt, 5, group_id);
      sqlite3_bind_text(stmt, 6, [[NSString stringWithFormat:@"%@", attr] UTF8String], -1,
NULL);

    }
    if (sqlite3_step(stmt) != SQLITE_DONE)
      NSLog(@"Error updating table links %d",site_id);
    sqlite3_finalize(stmt);
  }

  else {  // update existing row
```

```
        update = "UPDATE Links set name=?, link=?, rank=?, group_id=?, attributes=? WHERE
id=?";
        if (sqlite3_prepare_v2(database, update, -1, &stmt, nil) == SQLITE_OK) {
            sqlite3_bind_text(stmt, 1, [name UTF8String], -1, NULL);
            sqlite3_bind_text(stmt, 2, [site UTF8String], -1, NULL);
            sqlite3_bind_int(stmt, 3, rank);
            sqlite3_bind_int(stmt, 4, group_id);
            sqlite3_bind_text(stmt, 5, [attr UTF8String], -1, NULL);
            sqlite3_bind_int(stmt, 6, site_id);
        }
        if (sqlite3_step(stmt) != SQLITE_DONE) NSLog(@"Error updating table links");
        sqlite3_finalize(stmt);
    }
```

```
    update = "commit;";
    if (sqlite3_exec (database,update,NULL, NULL, &errorMsg) != SQLITE_OK) {NSLog(@"Error
creating table: %s", errorMsg);}

    sqlite3_close(database);
    return site_id;
}
-(int)sitesInsertUpdate:(NSString *)name :(NSString *)site :(int)site_id :(int)rank :(int)group_id
:(NSString *)attr :(id)obj {
    site_id=[self sitesDBInsertUpdate:name :site :site_id :rank :group_id :attr];
    return site_id;
}
```

We use a begin and commit (see later in the code) to process the SQL as transactions that can be rolled back. This makes the SQL execute much more rapidly as well as provide the ability to *not* commit if an error was made.

If site_id = 0 then we will insert a new record, otherwise we will update the existing record's name and other website information. On an insert we first do a select on the Links table key and then add one to get the next available key to create a new record. So if the Links table has a maximum id currently = 56 then the new record will be inserted with id=57.

The call to *sitesInsertObject* needs to be added to the *setValue* method within **Sites.m** as below. Because a site_id is generated for a new record within the database logic we need code to update our screen data structure *sitesData* which stores the site_id. This is done within the following method, *updateSiteid* which will be called after the database insert/update routine, *sitesInsertUpdate,* is called.

```
-(void)updateSiteid :(int)site_id {
    if ([sitesData count]>curRow) {
        NSDictionary *rowdata = [self.sitesData objectAtIndex:curRow];
        NSDictionary *row1=[[NSDictionary alloc] initWithObjectsAndKeys:[NSNumber
numberWithInt:site_id],@"id",[rowdata objectForKey:@"name"], @"name",[rowdata
objectForKey:@"group_id"], @"group_id",[NSNumber numberWithInt:curRank], @"rank",[rowdata
```

```
objectForKey:@"site"],@"site",[rowdata objectForKey:@"attributes"],@"attributes",nil];
      [self.sitesData replaceObjectAtIndex:curRow withObject:row1];
   }
}
```

```
-(void)setValue :(NSString *)aname :(NSString *)asite :(int)rank :(int)group_id :(int)arow
:(NSString *)attr {
   //update data in arow object dictionary
   NSDictionary *rowdata = [self.sitesData objectAtIndex:arow];
   int site_id=[[rowdata objectForKey:@"id"] integerValue];
   NSDictionary *row1=[[NSDictionary alloc] initWithObjectsAndKeys:[NSNumber
numberWithInt:site_id],@"id",aname, @"name",[NSNumber numberWithInt:rank], @"rank",
[NSNumber numberWithInt:group_id], @"group_id", asite,@"site", attr, @"attributes",nil];
   [self.sitesData replaceObjectAtIndex:arow withObject:row1];
```

```
   if (![asite isEqualToString:@""]) {
      curRank=rank;
      curRow=arow;
      site_id=[aData sitesInsertUpdate:aname :asite :site_id :rank :group_id :attr :self];
      [self updateSiteid:site_id];
   }
}
```

Add the variables *curRow* and *curRank* to the **sites.h** file.
@interface Sites : UITableViewController

```
{
   int curRow;
   int curRank;
```

 Run the app and test inserting and deleting new websites. Close the app then re-run
and the websites added or removed should appear. If your new records do not
appear and only the default records appear then check your code and re-try.

Bookmark Web Page

Now that we can save websites, we can add functionality to allow the user to quickly add the current webpage displayed in our Browser screen by calling the *sitesInsertObject* function we just added. When the user goes back to the *Sites* page the new link(s) will be displayed.

Copy the following code logic to implement the "Add Bookmark" feature to the Browser screen. We will be adding a '+' icon to the upper left in the viewer web browser code that will allow us to bookmark web site pages being viewed. This icon should not appear when browsing websites listed in the sites screen but should appear when we display the Browser screen from the TabBar—even though both functions use the same viewer object to display a web browser.

 Within AppDelegate.m modify the browser method call to setViewType to set to 0 so that a new type 1 which will specify for the viewer object to allow the "Add Bookmark" feature and show a "+" button in the top of the screen to allow the user to tap the feature.

```
viewController2.Url=[NSURL URLWithString:@"http://www.google.com"];
[viewController2 setViewType:1];
```

Insert at the top of viewer.m:
```
#import "viewer.h"
#import "DataAccess.h"
```

After the @synthesize statement create a variable, aData, to point to the DataAccess object.

```
@synthesize webView,Url,busy_image;
DataAccess *aData1;
```

Within the viewer.m *viewDidLoad* method add at the bottom. Note this code is very reuseable to add buttons to navigation bars for your apps.
```
//set add link button
aData1 = [[DataAccess alloc] init];
if (viewType==1) {
    self.navigationItem.leftBarButtonItem = [[UIBarButtonItem alloc]
initWithBarButtonSystemItem: UIBarButtonSystemItemAdd target:self
action:@selector(addAction:)];
    }
```

Add the function below after the *viewDidLoad* method. It will extract the current web page URL and title from the browser object *webView* and pass these to be inserted into our database Links table as a new website record. Note the logic at the end of the code to post an alert message to the user telling him the link was added.

```
#pragma mark - Sites logic to save website links

-(IBAction)addAction:(id)sender {
    //add link to sites local or remote database
    NSString *theTitle=[webView stringByEvaluatingJavaScriptFromString:@"document.title"];
    NSString *currentUrl = [webView
stringByEvaluatingJavaScriptFromString:@"window.location.href"];
    NSLog(@"URL:%@ and title:%@",currentUrl,theTitle);

    //insert website into local database or remote collaborative database
    int site_id=[aData1 sitesInsertUpdate:theTitle :currentUrl :0 :0 :0 :@"" :self];

    //Notify user link was added
    UIAlertController * alert=  [UIAlertController
                        alertControllerWithTitle:@"Add Bookmark"
                        message:[NSString stringWithFormat:@"Your bookmark for site %@ was
added.",theTitle]
                        preferredStyle:UIAlertControllerStyleAlert];
    UIAlertAction* ok = [UIAlertAction
                actionWithTitle:@"OK"
                style:UIAlertActionStyleDefault
                handler:^(UIAlertAction * action)
                { [alert dismissViewControllerAnimated:YES completion:nil]; }];
    [alert addAction:ok]; // add action to uialertcontroller
    [self presentViewController:alert animated:YES completion:nil];
}
```

Call sitesInsertUpdate, the routine to write out the new website record.

Run the app and test both the delete, update, and insert of websites in the Sites and Detail screens as well as adding bookmarks. The screens below shows a new website added via the "+" bookmark feature in the Browser screen.

Chapter 9: Server Usage and an RSS Reader Example

Now we get to the power sections of the book. Our app, storing its own data on the device is functional but limited. With the exchange of data with server-based processes and databases we can extend the power of the app one-hundred fold. We can use external servers in the following ways:

- RSS (Really Simple Syndication) data feeds are websites made to send XML data content and are easy to access from iOS. The example in this section is of this type.

- Screen scraping – pulling data from HTML screens by searching for tags and related content. This data transfer method isn't as 'clean' as RSS as the code is dependent on tags within the HTML which may be modified beyond our control. This book does not show this approach but the code to do it would take advantage of server access routines similar to the RSS example but the result would need to be parsed manually versus using XML parsers built into XCode such as in the RSS example.

- Web services are server based scripts, or code, that are intended to be called from 'client' applications on other servers, PC's and mobile devices. They execute a single piece of work and are purposefully built to support web-based *services*. Chapter 10 in the book will show how PHP server-based scripts can be easily used to create funtcions that connect and insert or retrieve data from a remote database. This is extremely powerful as it makes our app collaborative since multiple users of the app will share a single remote database—all users will be working with and sharing the same data and websites.

Extracting Server Data

The **NSURL** object is provided by iOS to handle server requests. It will call the website http://rss.cnn.com/rss/cnn_topstories.rss via its URL (Universal Record Locator) and the resulting data (usually HTML scripts or XML data) is passed back as a response.

We will implement the *NSURL* object below to call the CNN top stories RSS feed and then use a free third-party XML parsing library called *TouchXML* to parse the results. We will create a new TableView screen using the StoryBoard approach to creating screens to display the

RSS data we parse. Example output is shown to the right. Note that the feature we create will be able to parse most RSS feeds as the title and description tags are the same in most feeds.

Storyboards

We will create a new *UITableViewController* screen called *NewsFeed* to display our RSS results. This screen will be called from the *Sites* screen when the user taps on a RSS website.

1 First, to create the *NewsFeed* screen go to **File**, **New/File** and select **"User Interface"** on the left and select **"Storyboard"** and **Next**. Then type the name "NewsFeed" and click the **Create** button. Then go to **File**, **New/File** again and select **"Source"** on the left and **"Cocoa Touch Class"** and **Next**. Then select type *UITableViewController* with name "NewsFeed" and <u>no</u> xib file.

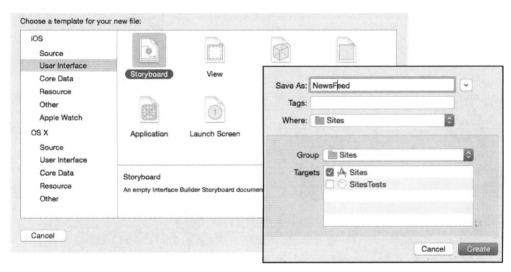

2 The following steps will create a StoryBoard with two screens that will look like the image below. The left screen, a UITableViewController, will display a list of all RSS content rows and the right screen will contain a web browser to show the detail of an RSS entry when we tap on it—basically, the RSS row has a link that we can click on to get the article details.

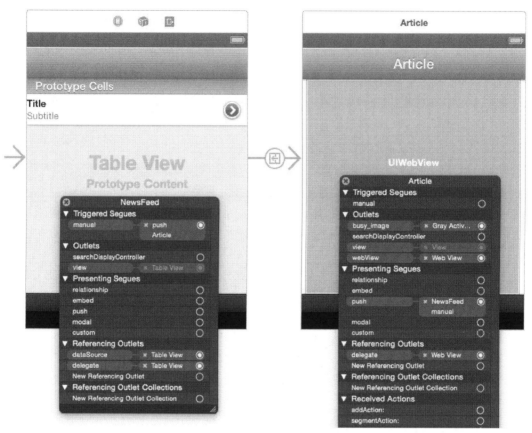

A. Click on the *NewsFeed.storyboard* file to bring up interface builder

B. Add a *TableViewController* by drag-dropping one from the object library on the right panel to the blank panel (your storyboard area) that is to the right of the panel marked "No Scenes." Click on the *TableViewController* and the Identity Inspector as shown to the right and type Class: **NewsFeed**.

C. While on the TableViewController select the File Inspector icon and check "Use Auto Layout" off and click on "Disable Size Classes" from the dialog that will appear.

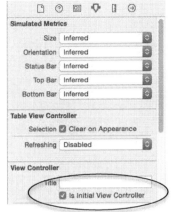

D. Click on the *Attributes Inspector* as shown to the right and click on "Is Initial View Controller".

E. Create a *View Controller* with a *Web View* within it as pictured above on the right. Go to the Identify Inspector for the View Controller just added and make sure it is of Class: **viewer**. This will be our web browser screen.

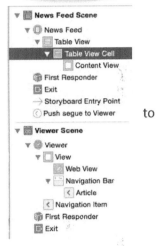

F. Drag a *Nagivation Bar* to the *View Controller* right above the Web View (you may have to size the web view down from the top to make sure the navigation bar is on top of the view) and type "Article" as the title on its' navigation item.

G. The white box underneath the text "Prototype Cells" in the TableView is a Table Cell. Control-click the Table Cell and drag the View Controller screen. Answer "Push" to the segue question. This creates a segue or navigation link from the Table View which is our list of RSS texts and display of a specific article using a web browser when we tap that article. The structure of the storyboard on the left of the Interface Builder should look like the image to the right including the "Push segue to Viewer" option just added.

H. Click on the seque arrow connecting the two screens and click on the Attributes Inspector as shown below and type Identifier="ViewArticle".

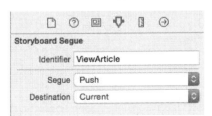

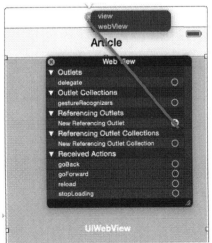

I. Right click on the *UIWebView* control to bring up the Web View properties screen as shown to the right. Drag-drop from the "New Referencing Outlet" circle to the yellow file owner icon as shown in the image to the right. Select "webView".

3

The code below adds a call from the Sites screen to our new Newsfeed screen which will display the RSS results. Insert at the top of **Sites.m** the new *Newsfeed.h* header file and then modify the other methods as shown below.

```
#import "Sites.h"
#import "viewer.h"
#import "Detail.h"
#import "Newsfeed.h"

- (void)tableView:(UITableView *)tableView didSelectRowAtIndexPath:(NSIndexPath *)indexPath
{
    NSUInteger row = [indexPath row];
    NSDictionary *rowdata = [self.sitesData objectAtIndex:row];
    NSString *attr=[rowdata objectForKey:@"attributes"];
    curRow=row;
    NSString *astr=@"";
    if ([attr rangeOfString:@"rss"].location==NSNotFound) {
        viewer *controller = [[viewer alloc] initWithNibName:@"viewer" bundle:nil];
        controller.Url=[NSURL URLWithString:[rowdata objectForKey:@"site"]];
        [controller setViewType:0];
        controller.navigationItem.title=@"Browser";
        [self.navigationController pushViewController:controller animated:YES];
    }
    else {
        UIStoryboard *newsfeed = [UIStoryboard storyboardWithName:@"NewsFeed" bundle:nil];
        NewsFeed *viewController3 = [newsfeed instantiateInitialViewController];
        viewController3.title=@"RSS Feed";
        viewController3.url=[rowdata objectForKey:@"site"];
        [self.navigationController pushViewController:viewController3 animated:YES];
    }
}
```

At this point you will have an error in the code saying the URL property isn't available. You need to complete the coding in the next section for this to be resovled.

Server Requests

The NSURL object is provided by iOS to handle server URL requests. It will call the URL and the resulting data (usually HTML scripts or XML data) is stored and can be used in your code.

Newsfeed will be coded to call the RSS server based on the website URL and parse the XML results into an array to display them in its UITableView object.

 The following methods should be added to the **Newsfeed.h** file to handle the server call and retrieve the response XML into the variable *xmlData*.

```
@interface NewsFeed : UITableViewController
{
    NSMutableArray *List;          //Hold the list of entries for the uitableview
    NSMutableData *xmlData;
    NSString *url;
}

@property(nonatomic,retain)NSMutableArray *List;
@property(nonatomic,retain)NSMutableData *xmlData;
@property(nonatomic,retain)NSString *url;
```

Add the code below to the top of **NewsFeed.m,** replaceing the existing *viewDidLoad* method, to get the screen going and call the server to get the data we need.

```
#import "NewsFeed.h"
#import "viewer.h"
#import "TouchXML.h"

@implementation NewsFeed
@synthesize List, xmlData, url;

#pragma mark - View lifecycle

- (void)viewDidLoad
{
    [super viewDidLoad];
    [self LoadNewsFeedRequest:url];
}

//When cell is clicked go to the webbrowser in the storyboard
- (void)prepareForSegue:(UIStoryboardSegue *)segue sender:(id)sender
{
    if([segue.identifier isEqualToString:@"ViewArticle"])
    {
        NSIndexPath *row = sender;
        viewer *view = [segue destinationViewController];
        view.Url=[NSURL URLWithString:[[List objectAtIndex:row.row] objectForKey:@"link"]];
        [view setViewType:0];
        view.navigationItem.title=@"Browser";
```

```objc
    }
  }

-(void)LoadNewsFeedRequest:(NSString *)aurl
{
  if (xmlData!=nil)
    xmlData=nil;
  if (xmlData==nil)
    xmlData = [[NSMutableData alloc] init];

  NSURL *url = [NSURL URLWithString:aurl];
  NSURLRequest* request = [NSURLRequest requestWithURL:url
                          cachePolicy:NSURLRequestUseProtocolCachePolicy
                        timeoutInterval:180.0];
  NSURLConnection *rssConnection = [[NSURLConnection alloc]
                    initWithRequest:request delegate:self];
}

- (void)Connection:(NSURLConnection *)connection didFailWithError:(NSError *)error {
  NSLog(@"Request failed: %d",error.code);

  UIAlertController * alert=  [UIAlertController
                alertControllerWithTitle:@"No Connectivity"
                message:@"Failed RSS Request"
                preferredStyle:UIAlertControllerStyleAlert];

  UIAlertAction* ok = [UIAlertAction
          actionWithTitle:@"OK"
          style:UIAlertActionStyleDefault
          handler:^(UIAlertAction * action)
          {
            [alert dismissViewControllerAnimated:YES completion:nil];
          }];
  [alert addAction:ok]; // add action to uialertcontroller
  [self presentViewController:alert animated:YES completion:nil];
}

// Called when a chunk of data has been downloaded.
- (void)connection:(NSURLConnection *)connection didReceiveData:(NSData *)data {
  // Append the downloaded chunk of data.
  [self.xmlData appendData:data];
  //   NSString *astr=[[NSString alloc] initWithData:data encoding:NSUTF8StringEncoding];
  //   NSLog(@"RSS String %d %@",data.length,astr);
}

- (void)connectionDidFinishLoading:(NSURLConnection *)connection {
  //  NSString *astr = [[NSString alloc] initWithData:getData encoding:NSUTF8StringEncoding];
  //  NSLog(@"RSS String %d %@",getData.length,astr);
  [self ParseNewsFeed];
}
```

This code will be called to display the detail viewer web browser on a single RSS entry in the table view. This is called a 'seque' in Storyboard language—when you transition to another screen.

 This code takes the aurl string variable passed to the method and issues an asynchronous server request. Asynchronous means that the code will not wait for the completion but yield control back to the main screen. In the background the server request is still running and it is up to our code to load and refresh the table view when the server reply is received.

 This method, *didFailWithError*, will only be called if the server request fails. If it does an alert message is displayed.

 didReceiveData method is called by the server code every time it receives data and just appends the data to the variable xmlData.

The *connectionDidFinishLoading* method is called when the final data is received. We then call *ParseNewsFeed* to parse the results and display the results in the table view.

Parse XML

RSS XML is returned as data from the server call above and has a standardized format so that each entry (each news story in our example) will have a Title, Link, and Description with the corresponding tags: <title>, <link> and <description>. Here is an example of the a news story in XML. The tag for each story is <item>. The text our parser will retrieve for the title, link, and description is underlined:

```
<item>
<title>Bill to allow guns on campus awaits Texas governor's signature</title>
<guid isPermaLink="false">http://www.cnn.com/2015/06/01/us/texas-legislature-passes-campus-
carry-guns/index.html</guid>
<link>http://rss.cnn.com/~r/rss/cnn_topstories/~3/n0PPI2fAEaQ/index.html</link>
<description>The Texas Legislature has voted to allow guns within buildings on public college
campuses throughout the state.<div class="feedflare"><a
href="http://rss.cnn.com/~ff/rss/cnn_topstories?a=n0PPI2fAEaQ:MU8Ej440KoM:yll2AUoC8zA"><
img src="http://feeds.feedburner.com/~ff/rss/cnn_topstories?d=yll2AUoC8zA"
border="0"></img></a> ...
</item>
```

iOS has a library that helps us parse and read XML but we will use a third-party library called *TouchXML* that is even easier to use.

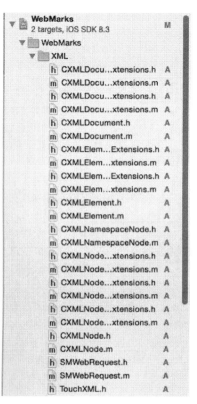

The following method will parse through the data returned from the server call (stored in self.xmlData) and create an array, *List*, of data dictionaries which each contain one news story.

 To add the third-party code *TouchXML* you should right-click on the **WebMarks** project and select **New Group** and name it **XML**. Then right-click on the new XML folder and select **Add Files to WebMarks** and navigate to the *WebMarks_Book/XML* folder. Select all files within and make sure you select "**Copy items if needed**" option. This should copy these files to your project. See image to the right.

Click on **WebMarks** project again and on the right click on **Build Settings**. Click **All** and in the search, type "**Header search**" and press **Enter**. Edit the Header Search Paths by double-clicking on it and add the following entry by pressing the '+' button to get a new entry: "$(SDKROOT)/usr/include/libxml2". The result should be as below:

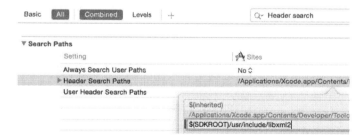

Now click on **Build Phases** and open "**Compile Sources**". Edit each file starting with "CXML" and the "SMWebRequest.m" file by double-clicking to the right of the file under the "Compiler Flags" option and type "**-fno-objc-arc**". We do this to disable the ARC (automatic reference counting) complie option as this XML parsing code needs this to compile.

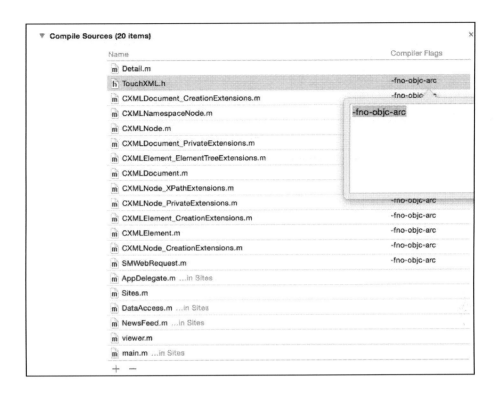

6 Add the following routine to Newsfeed.m to parse the XML results into the *List* data array.

```
-(void)ParseNewsFeed
{
  CXMLDocument *wirexml = [[CXMLDocument alloc] initWithData:self.xmlData options:0
error:nil];
  //   NSString *astr = [[NSString alloc] initWithData:self.xmlData
encoding:NSWindowsCP1252StringEncoding];
  //   NSLog(@"ParseRSS Data:%@",astr);

  NSArray *nodes = [wirexml nodesForXPath:@"//item" error:nil];
  NSMutableArray *list = [[NSMutableArray alloc] init];
  NSMutableDictionary *entry;
  for(CXMLElement *node in nodes)
  {
    entry = [[NSMutableDictionary alloc] init];
    /*  for (int index = 0; index<[node childCount]; index++) {
         NSLog(@"%d:%@",index, [[node childAtIndex:index] stringValue]); //output
       }
    */
    NSString *title = [[[node elementsForName:@"title"] objectAtIndex:0] stringValue];
    NSString *link = [[[node elementsForName:@"link"] objectAtIndex:0] stringValue];
```

```
            NSString *desc = [[[node elementsForName:@"description"] objectAtIndex:0] stringValue];

            //Ensure description is just the text (not extra HTML code)
            NSInteger loc=[desc rangeOfString:@"<"].location;
            if ((loc<=0) || (loc>100000))
                desc=@"";
            else if (loc>0)
                desc=[desc substringToIndex:loc];

            [entry setObject:title forKey:@"title"];
            [entry setObject:link forKey:@"link"];
            [entry setObject:desc forKey:@"description"];
            [list addObject:entry];
        }
        List = list;
        [self.tableView reloadData];
    }
```

A   *CXMLDocument* is the object class that will parse our XML and we initialize it with our *xmlData* reply from the server here. xmlData is an NSMutableData object that holds all of the data returned from the RSS feed server call.

B   *nodesForXPath* parses the XML and loads the array *nodes* using the string "//item" to put each item tag within each node array object. The code then loops through each node and we will be adding one entry into our list NSMutableData object for each node processed.

C   The method *elementsForName* will search within the node string and pull out the string related to the tag "title", "link" and "description". These strings contain the text we want to save within our *list* data structure so we contruct a NSMutableDictionary, put these three strings in it and then use *addObject* to add this NSMutableDictionary named *entry* to our *list* object.

D   Finally we will reload the table view which will create one table cell (Row) per entry in the list array we just created.

Custom TableView Cells

Up until now we have used standard cells for each row of our talbe but we will now create a *custom* tableview cell .xlb interface file to display the RSS results in our NewsFeed table view. Using **File, New/File** menu select the type: **User Interface/Empty** as below. Press **Next** and then name the file **WireCell** when the dialog appears asking for a name.

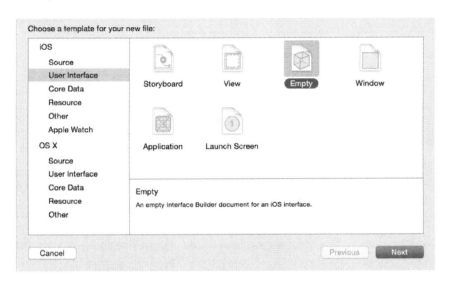

Select the new **WireCell.xlb** file from the project file list and Interface Builder should appear. Select the object type "**Table View Cell**" and drag it into the main interface builder area. Create two labels as shown below and make sure to set their **Tag** properties to 1, for the top label, and 2 for the bottom label. Save this file.

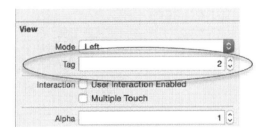

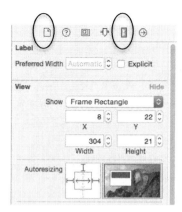

8 For WireCell tap on the File inspector (the first circle on the properties bar in the image on the right) and set **Auto Layout off**. Then click on the Size Inspector (shown to the right) and make the **Autoresizing** look like the picture with four red arrows highlighted. This allows the labels to size to the width of the device they are in. In the Attributes Inspector for the 2nd label set the font size to 14 and "Lines" to 0 to allow any number of text lines to wrap.

9 Add the following tableView methods to NewsFeed.m to display the RSS data.

```objc
- (NSInteger)numberOfSectionsInTableView:(UITableView *)tableView
{
    // Return the number of sections.
    return 1;
}

- (NSInteger)tableView:(UITableView *)tableView numberOfRowsInSection:(NSInteger)section
{

    // Return the number of rows in the section.
    return List.count;

} - (UITableViewCell *)tableView:(UITableView *)tableView cellForRowAtIndexPath:(NSIndexPath *)indexPath
{
    static NSString *CellIdentifier = @"WireCell";     //get the name of the custom cell

    UITableViewCell *cell = [tableView dequeueReusableCellWithIdentifier:CellIdentifier];
    if (cell == nil) {
       cell = [[[NSBundle mainBundle] loadNibNamed:@"WireCell" owner:self options:nil] lastObject];
    }

    // Configure the cell...
    NSMutableDictionary *item = [List objectAtIndex:indexPath.row];
    [(UILabel *)[cell viewWithTag:1] setText:[item objectForKey:@"title"]]; //add the title to the cell

    UILabel *alab=(UILabel *)[cell viewWithTag:2];
    [alab setText:[item objectForKey:@"description"]];        //add the description to the cell.
    alab.lineBreakMode = NSLineBreakByWordWrapping;

    return cell;
}

- (void)tableView:(UITableView *)tableView didSelectRowAtIndexPath:(NSIndexPath *)indexPath
{
    [self performSegueWithIdentifier: @"ViewArticle" sender: indexPath];
}
```

Note the use of the custom cell *WireCell* in the code and the alternative method of accessing controls in this custom cell by using the *viewWithTag* method on the cell object. This is why it was important to set tags to 1 and 2 on the controls when creating the custom cell.

Run the app and select the "CNN Top Stories" website and you should see the following. Click a story entry and the browser screen should appear.

Sizing TableView Cells Dynamically

 Because the RSS news stories are of various lengths of text a static height for our cells will not work. The following code should be added to Newsfeed.m to make sure each cell has its height dynamically sized to fit the entire description of the article—which varies by row displayed.

```
-(int)getTextHeight:(int)arow {
    NSDictionary *rowdata = [List objectAtIndex:arow];
    int width=295;  //320 normal iphone, landscape: 5:568, <5.0:480
    if ((self.interfaceOrientation==UIInterfaceOrientationLandscapeLeft) ||
(self.interfaceOrientation==UIInterfaceOrientationLandscapeRight)) {
        if ([ [ UIScreen mainScreen ] bounds ].size.height==568) {
            width=543;
        }
        else {
            width=455;
        }
    }
    CGSize constraint = CGSizeMake(width, 20000.0f);
    CGSize size = [[rowdata objectForKey:@"description"] sizeWithFont:[UIFont
fontWithName:@"Helvetica" size:(CGFloat)14.0] constrainedToSize:constraint
lineBreakMode:UILineBreakModeWordWrap];
    NSLog(@"***Height: %0f.0 Text%@",size.height, [rowdata objectForKey:@"description"]);
    return size.height;
}


- (CGFloat)tableView:(UITableView *)tableView heightForRowAtIndexPath:(NSIndexPath
*)indexPath
{
    NSUInteger aindex = [indexPath row];
    int height=[self getTextHeight :aindex];
    // NSLog( @"heightForRowAtIndexPath aindex: %d, row: %d, height: %d", aindex, [indexPath
row],height);
    return height+25;
}


- (UITableViewCell *)tableView:(UITableView *)tableView cellForRowAtIndexPath:(NSIndexPath
*)indexPath
{
. . .


    CGRect aframe=alab.frame;
    NSLog(@"cell width:%0f.0  %0f.0",cell.frame.size.width,aframe.origin.y);
    aframe.size.height=[self getTextHeight :[indexPath row]];
    [alab setFrame:aframe];


    return cell;
}
```

Calculate the *description* text height using the method *sizeWithFont.* This is key to the whole routine as once we know its height we can change the height of the cell frame to accommodate the text height needed. Note that heightForRowAtIndexPath method is a standard UITableView method that we override to change a cell's height.

Run the app again and select the "CNN Top Stories" and you should now see each cell size to fit the entire description text.

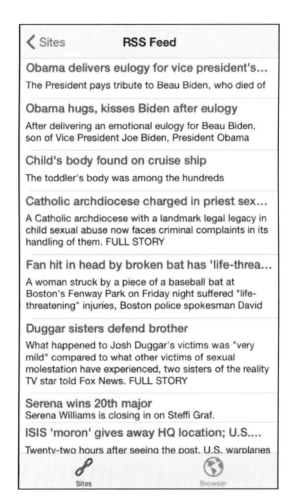

Chapter 10: Server Databases

The real power of mobile apps comes with accessing cloud (web) server processes or *web services*. This allows massive data and processing to be provided to small mobile devices...lots of power and data available *anywhere*. This is what makes apps so powerful and allows collaboration between users of apps. In this chapter we will add code to store our data on a remote server database. Since everyone with the app will access the same database it allows all users to share websites with each other—a lot more interesting than keeping track of only our own websites.

Creating the Database

For this sample app we will be using a MySQL database located on the author's Ray of Light Software company's server. On this server is a MySQL database named **sites,** shown below. To create a table within a database you can use a visual database tool as shown below or execute a SQL *Create* statement such as the one shown below that created the Links table.

```
CREATE TABLE Links (
      id INT,
      group_id INT,
      name VARCHAR(50),
      link VARCHAR(4048),
      attributes VARCHAR(20),
      rank INT,
   rankCount INT
);
```

Database tool on my website showing the **sites** database and table *Links*:

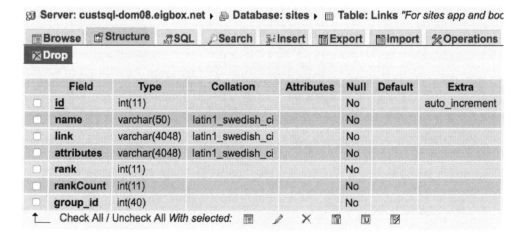

Example rows within the Links table:

			id	owner	name	link	attributes	rank
☐	✎ Edit	✕ Delete	1	0	CNN	http://www.cnn.com		0
☐	✎ Edit	✕ Delete	5	0	CS Monitor	http://www.csmonitor.com		0
↑	Check All / Uncheck All *With selected:*		✎	✕	🗐			

Remote Database: Querying records and extracting data

There are three PHP scripts on the website to extract, insert, or delete data from the Links table. PHP is a server-side scripting language to build server services such as database access and data exchange as we are doing. This will support our app and replace the SQLite local database approach to storing data.   The website URL to call to extract data is maintained by the author at the URL: http://rayoflightsoftware.com/sites/Links_get_children.php
and the script follows (you do not need to type this script in but in the future you may want to build similar scripts and put them on your website for your apps). "echo" is the output statement that will formulate an XML return string to our app.

PHP Script: **Links_get_children.php**

```php
<?php
$con = mysql_connect("dalematheny.domaincommysql.com","damath","sites");
if (!$con)
  {
  die('Could not connect: ' . mysql_error());
  }

mysql_select_db("sites", $con);

$result = mysql_query("SELECT id,group_id,name,link,attributes,rank FROM Links where
group_id=$_GET[group_id] order by rank Desc, name");

echo "<records>";

while($row = mysql_fetch_array($result))
{
  echo "<record>";
  echo "<id>" . $row['id'] . "</id>" . "<group_id>" . $row['group_id'] . "</group_id>" . "<name>" .
$row['name'] . "</name>" . "<link>" . $row['link'] . "</link>" . "<attributes>" . $row['attributes'] .
"</attributes>" . "<rank>" . $row['rank'] . "</rank>";
  echo "</record>";
}

echo "</records>";

mysql_close($con);
?>
```

1 Before adding code to support this PHP script, we need to add a routine to call our server using the SMWEBRequest object. Note this is a streamlined free third-party object that we will use instead of NSURL, the iOS default server access object. Using SMWEBRequest is easier than NSURL. To add support for this object add the following import statements at the top of **DataAccess.m** and then add the code given.

```
#import "DataAccess.h"
#import "SMWEBRequest.h"
#import "TouchXML.h"
#import "Sites.h"

@implementation DataAccess
Sites *sitesDelegate;
```

A
```
- (void)requestError:(NSError *)theError {
    NSLog(@"Error: %@",[NSString stringWithFormat:@"%@",[theError localizedDescription]]);
    UIAlertView *alertView = [[UIAlertView alloc] initWithTitle:@"Server Error"
                                message:[theError localizedDescription] delegate:self
    cancelButtonTitle:@"Cancel" otherButtonTitles:nil];
    [alertView show];
}
```

```
-(void)GetDataToParse:(NSString *)url         //The Url to get the data from
              :(NSString *)methodName         //The name of the method that is going to parse the
data
              :(id)obj
{
```
B
```
    SMWebRequest *termRequest = [SMWebRequest requestWithURL:[NSURL
URLWithString:url]];
    NSLog(@"Request> %@",url);
```
C
```
    [termRequest addTarget:obj action:NSSelectorFromString(methodName)
forRequestEvents:SMWebRequestEventComplete];
    [termRequest addTarget:obj action:NSSelectorFromString(@"requestError:")
forRequestEvents:SMWebRequestEventError];
    [termRequest start];
}
```

A Use an UIAlertView to quickly show an error message to report server connectivity or other system error related to the server request call made in the GetDataToParse routine.

B the method *requestWithURL* starts the asynchronous server request with the url string passed to the method.

C The addTarget method sets up both error handling and successful return methods. One will be called when the server request finishes. Note the object the methods can be called in does not have to be the DataAccess object but could be the Sites screen or other object that is passed into the routine in the *obj* variable.

2 Code to insert into *DataAccess.m to call the Links_get_children script and parse the results. Replace* the sitesLoad routine with:

A

```
-(void)sitesLoad:(NSMutableArray *)linksarray :(int)group_id :(id)obj{
   if (kDataType==2)
      [self sitesDBLoad:linksarray :group_id];
   else if (kDataType==3)
      [self sitesRemoteLoad :group_id :obj];
}
```

B

```
-(void)sitesRemoteLoad :(int)group_id :(id)obj
{
   NSString *requestString = [NSString
stringWithFormat:@"http://rayoflightsoftware.com/sites/Links_get_children.php?group_id=%d",gr
oup_id];
   sitesDelegate=obj;
   [self GetDataToParse:requestString :@"parseData:" :self];
}
```

C

```
-(void)parseData:(NSData *)data {
   //Prepare parsing of xml.
      NSString *astr = [[NSString alloc] initWithData:data
encoding:NSWindowsCP1252StringEncoding];
      NSLog(@"Data:%@",astr);

   NSMutableArray *linksarray=[NSMutableArray new];
   CXMLDocument *doc = [[CXMLDocument alloc] initWithData:data options:0 error:nil];
   NSString *aname=@"";
   NSString *alink=@"";
   NSString *attr=@"";

   //id, name, rank, site/link, attributes
   NSDictionary *row1;
   NSArray *nodes = [doc nodesForXPath:@"//record" error:nil];
   for (CXMLElement *node in nodes) {
      aname=[[node childAtIndex:2] stringValue];
      alink=[[node childAtIndex:3] stringValue];
      attr=[[node childAtIndex:4] stringValue];

      row1=[[NSDictionary alloc] initWithObjectsAndKeys:
         [NSNumber numberWithInt:[[[node childAtIndex:0] stringValue] integerValue]],@"id",
         [NSNumber numberWithInt:[[[node childAtIndex:5] stringValue] integerValue]],@"rank",
         [NSNumber numberWithInt:[[[node childAtIndex:1] stringValue]
integerValue]],@"group_id",
         aname, @"name", alink, @"site", attr, @"attributes", nil];
      [linksarray addObject:row1];
   }

   [sitesDelegate reLoadSites:linksarray];
}
```

This code adds the option, if the *kDataType* contstant=3, to call remote access PHP scripts instead of SQLite database calls to get data. Note that since all code is encapsulated within the DataAccess file and the method *sitesLoad* is already being called by the Sites screen, the rest of our application doesn't change—we just need to modify the DataAccess code to pull data from a server instead of a local database. This is why we created routines such as *sitesLoad:* so that we can have a 'data layer' of code separate from our interface and program logic—this is standard coding architecture practice for applications.

The code: [self GetDataToParse:requestString :@"parseData:" :self];
calls the server with our URL contained in *requestString* which for our select function is:

http://rayoflightsoftware.com/sites/Links_get_children.php?group_id=0

The code also specifies what method, *parseData*, should be called upon a successful return. The *self* variable tells the method that the *parseData* method is in the current DataAccess object.

The *parseData* method uses the *CXMLDocument* object to parse returning data. The data that returns must be parsed and then inserted into the the *linksarray* array. The XML data being parsed uses the tag *record* for each website and *id, name, rank, attributes, group_id, link* tags for each Links table record. Here is a sample XML string with two websites: *CNN* and *CS Monitor*.

```
<records><record><id>1</id><group_id>0</group_id><name>CNN</name><link>http://www.cnn
.com</link><attributes></attributes><rank>0</rank></record><record><id>18</id><group_id>0</
group_id><name>CS
Monitor</name><link>http://www.csmonitor.com</link><attributes></attributes><rank>4</rank></
record></records>
```

At the bottom of sites.h add the headers:
-(void)reLoadSites :(NSMutableArray *)sitesArray;
-(void)updateSiteid :(int)site_id;

Within sites.m the code below for the supporting routine *reloadSites* which is called after the *parseData* routine for the sitesLoad process above to refresh the list of sites.
```
- (void)reLoadSites :(NSMutableArray *)sitesArray {
   if (sitesArray!=nil) {
      if (self.sitesData!=nil) {
         [self.sitesData removeAllObjects];
         sitesData=nil;
      }
      sitesData=sitesArray;
   }
   [self.tableView reloadData];
}
```

90

Run the application and you should get all websites that are currently on the server—and there might be a lot as all readers of this book all share the same database!

Remote Database: Deleting Records

To delete a record we add new methods to the app's existing delete logic in DataAccess object.

PHP Script: **Links_delete.php**

```php
<?php
$con = mysql_connect("dalematheny.domaincommysql.com","damath","sites");
if (!$con)
  {
  die('Could not connect: ' . mysql_error());
  }

mysql_select_db("sites", $con);

  mysql_query("DELETE FROM Links WHERE id=$_GET[id]");

mysql_close($con);
?>
```

The code below should be added to the DataAccess.m delete record area. It replaces *sitesDelete*, already being called by the Sites screen, to now delete records on our remote sites database. No parsing or other action is required for a successful return.

```objc
-(void)responseDelete:(NSData *)data {
   NSString *astr = [[NSString alloc] initWithData:data
encoding:NSWindowsCP1252StringEncoding];
   NSLog(@"responseHttp:%@",astr);
}

-(void)sitesRemoteDelete:(int)aid :(id)obj
{
   //Server is rayoflightsoftware.com  66.96.162.201
   NSString *requestString = [NSString
stringWithFormat:@"http://rayoflightsoftware.com/sites/Links_delete.php?id=%d",aid];
   sitesDelegate=obj;
   [self GetDataToParse:requestString :@"responseDelete:" :self];
}

-(void)sitesDelete :(int)site_id :(id)obj {
   if (kDataType==2)
      [self sitesDBDelete:site_id];
   else if (kDataType==3)
      [self sitesRemoteDelete:site_id :obj];
}
```

Remote Database: Inserting and Updating Records

PHP Script **Links_update.php** for inserting and updating one website record. If the id=0 then we insert otherwise we update the record at the given id.

```php
<?php
$con = mysql_connect("dalematheny.domaincommysql.com","damath","sites");
if (!$con)
  {
  die('Could not connect: ' . mysql_error());
  }

mysql_select_db("sites", $con);

echo "<records>";
echo "<record>";

if ($_GET[id] == 0)
{
   $result = mysql_query("INSERT INTO Links (name, rank, rankCount, link, attributes, group_id)
VALUES ('$_GET[name]', $_GET[rank], 1, '$_GET[link]','$_GET[attributes]',$_GET[group_id] )");

   echo "<id>" . mysql_insert_id() . "</id>";
}
else
{
   $result = mysql_query("Update Links set link='$_GET[link]',
rank=(rank*rankcount+$_GET[rank])/(rankcount+1), rankcount=rankcount+1, name='$_GET[name]',
attributes='$_GET[attributes]', group_id=$_GET[group_id] where id=$_GET[id]");

   echo "<id>" . $_GET[id] . "</id>";
}

echo "</record>";
echo "</records>";

mysql_close($con);
?>
```

 Add the code below to allow the existing *sitesInsertUpdate* method to call our remote database.

```objc
-(int)sitesInsertUpdate:(NSString *)name :(NSString *)site :(int)site_id :(int)rank :(int)group_id
:(NSString *)attr :(id)obj {
   if (kDataType==2)
      site_id=[self sitesDBInsertUpdate:name :site :site_id :rank :group_id :attr];
   else if (kDataType==3)
      [self sitesRemoteInsertUpdate:name :(NSString *)site :site_id :rank :group_id :attr :obj];
   return site_id;
}

-(void)sitesRemoteInsertUpdate:(NSString *)aname :(NSString *)alink :(int)site_id :(int)rank
```

```
:(int)group_id :(NSString *)attr :(id)obj
{
    //Server is rayoflightsoftware.com 66.96.162.201
    NSString *requestString = [NSString
stringWithFormat:@"http://rayoflightsoftware.com/sites/Links_update.php?name=%@&id=%d&ra
nk=%d&link=%@&attributes=%@&group_id=%d",aname,site_id,rank,alink,attr,group_id];
    requestString=[requestString stringByReplacingOccurrencesOfString:@" " withString:@"+"];
    NSLog(@"Insert cell:%@",requestString);

    sitesDelegate=obj;
    //NSDictionary *rowdata = [self.sitesData objectAtIndex:curRow];
    [self GetDataToParse:requestString :@"afterupdate:" :self];
}

-(void)afterupdate:(NSData *)data {
    //parse and update site_id table id if from new inserted record
    //   NSString *astr = [[NSString alloc] initWithData:data
encoding:NSWindowsCP1252StringEncoding];
    //   NSLog(@"Data afterupdate:%@",astr);
    CXMLDocument *doc = [[CXMLDocument alloc] initWithData:data options:0 error:nil];
    NSArray *nodes = [doc nodesForXPath:@"//record" error:nil];
    CXMLElement *node=[nodes objectAtIndex:0];
    int aid=[[[node childAtIndex:0] stringValue] integerValue];
    [sitesDelegate updateSiteid:aid];
}
```

A — This code creates the calling HTTP string with parameters for all of our data that we pass to the routine to either update or insert a new website record.

B — This code calls the server and tells it to call routine afterupdate when complete. After completion the return string will have the new record id in a "record" tag. This id

C — is passed back to the Sites screen's *updateSiteid* method using the pointer to the Sites object: sitesDelegate that got passed into the *sitesRemoteInsertUpdate* method initially.

3 — Add the code below to the viewer.h header
```
-(void)updateSiteid :(int)site_id;
```

and viewer.m at the bottom of the file above the @end statement after the addAction method, the method that calls the remote server database call with its call:
```
int site_id=[aData sitesInsertUpdate:theTitle :currentUrl :0 :0 :0 :@"" :self];
```

```
-(void)updateSiteid :(int)site_id {
}
```

We don't need code here, just the method to support the remote server database logic.

Data scope using Remove Server calls

Look at the addAction method within the viewer.m file. The *scope* of the *aData* object variable within the viewer screen—it is declared at the screen level at the top of the viewer.m file. If we just declared it within the *addAction* method then the asynchronous nature of the remote server database call would crash the system.

Why? Trace through the flow: once the asynchronous remote call is made then the logic flows through the end of the addAction method and this would remove the *aData* object from memory before the remote server call is finished. Since the logic in DataAccess calls a method within DataAccess upon its successful return (the *afterupdate* method) there would be no object to go to since the DataAccess object was already removed from memory. So, we need to keep the scope of aData at the screen level and that is why we declared *aData* at the top of the screen and initialized the object in the *viewer.viewDidLoad* method.

 Run the application and test the add and delete of websites using the remote database server logic. When doing this if you have the WebMarks app downloaded from the App Store you should see all changes affecting all instances of WebMarks.

Chapter 11: Collaboration and Sharing Data

Since our database can now be shared by multiple users let's add a powerful group feature that will allow users to see only the groups and websites they are allowed to see. **This allows clubs, families, classes, etc. to establish groups of shared website links and makes our app into a social bookmarking application.**

 Exercise: Create the Groups Collaboration Feature
Design and code this group feature using the steps below. The database tables and PHP scripts needed are provided on the same server we used to store the websites and are shown below the instructions. Use Google if needed to find out how to code something. Just search for "Xcode" and the topic. If you want to design this feature yourself take some time to do this now. You can compare your design to my design below when finished. If you don't want to design this feature then read on now!

Design of Groups Feature
To add this capability we need to add several features:
1) We will take the approach that the WebMarks screen will show websites for a single group at a time—a currently selected group. Changes in code will be needed to ensure that only a currently selected groups' websites are visible.
2) a group screen which allows selecting a group (the currently active group) or create a new group. A new group will require a group passcode that can be shared with all members to allow access to a group

Example: if the user has the Global group_id=0 (all users should) and a group called Movies his Groups screen would appear with two entries:
> Global
> Movies

Another user, Jessica Jones, might have access to Global and a group called Jones Family and his groups screen would appear as:
> Global
> Jones Family

Note that the group name will need to be unique when created.

3) a unique member identification to allow us to only display groups that the user has the right to access. This member ID will be stored in a table that lists the user id and group_ids that the user has access to currently.

Given this design the following Database Tables, PHP scripts and coding changes will be needed.

Note that the Database tables and PHP scripts given below are already created and on the server.

Database Tables

We will need two new tables in our database: groups and members. These are specified as:

```
CREATE TABLE groups (
    group_id INT,
    name VARCHAR(50),
    code VARCHAR(20)
);

CREATE TABLE members (
    group_id INT,
    userid VARCHAR(50)
);
```

The *groups* table stores the groups with their id, name and security code and *members* table keeps atrack of all groups that each member has access to.

Coding

1. Modify DataAccess.h and DataAccess.m to call the PHP scripts for select, insert/update, and delete Group features. When finished, *each* of these functions should call the select PHP script so that an accurate set of groups is in memory. This select routine should in turn call back to the Groups screen to reload the display of the screen.

2. Modify the Sites.h and Sites.m code to

   a) add a "Groups" button in the upper right of the navigation bar (see the viewer.m *ViewDidLoad* method for an example). Use Google or the Apple reference code guides available online to see how to code this using a word in your button instead of a system button such as "Edit". Your method that is called when the Groups button is pressed should bring up the new Groups screen you will create.

   b) add logic to store the current group selected from the new Groups screen. Use this current group variable when saving website data (as opposed to the old group_id value set in the Detail screen) or when loading websites to display. Note that the current select websites database logic is already coded to pick websites with group=0 as shown in the code snippet already in your code:
   ```
   [aData sitesLoad:self.sitesData :0 :self]; //group=0 default group
   ```
   You will need to change this to pass in the currently selected group.

3. Change the detail screen: remove the 'Owner' picker view. We'll set the owner now as from

the new Groups screen.

4. Create a new Groups *UITextViewController* screen including .xib file. Add code in this to do the following:

a. Have a data structure to hold the data for the table (see Sites.h and .m).

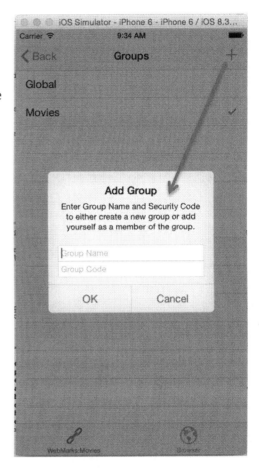

b. Write code (such as in the Detail.h and Detail.m screen) to access the DataAccess file. Write code to call the select groups PHP script code you wrote in step 1 within the DataAccess.m file.

c. Write code to set the current group id that can be called from the Sites screen when the Groups screen is created. Note the checkbox next to the currently selected row in the screen to the right.

d. Add table view code to display the rows. Add code to have a checkbox appear next to the current group that is being used by your Sites screen.

Note the code below will allow you to set a checkbox icon on or off for a row within the display logic:

```
if ([[rowdata objectForKey:@"group_id"] integerValue]==curGroup_id)
    cell.accessoryType=UITableViewCellAccessoryCheckmark;
else
    cell.accessoryType=UITableViewCellAccessoryNone;
```

e. Add table view code to handle a delete operation (the user can delete a row by swiping the row to the left). Add code to call the PHP delete group script: this code will call the DataAccess code you wrote in step (1).

f.   Add a "+" button in the upper right of the navigation bar of the screen. See code in viewer.m where we did this for this screen. The code should allow you to add an existing group or create a new group. Use an UIAlertController with text entry fields to gather the information. The screen above shows what this dialog box might look like. Note it accepts input for both a group name and passcode as we want access to groups passcode protected. The group creator should get to set this code when creating a group and only give it out to people he wants to access the group. When a user adds a group to his list of available groups he must use the passcode to access it.

PHP Scripts

The three scripts needed are blow as groups_get_children, groups_update and groups_delete:

http://rayoflightsoftware.com/sites/groups_get_children.php

The groups_get_children below code will use the input of the unique userid and return all groups the user has been given access to. The global group_id=0 is always returned.

```php
<?php
$con = mysql_connect("dalematheny.domaincommysql.com","damath","sites");
if (!$con)
  {
  die('Could not connect: ' . mysql_error());
  }

mysql_select_db("sites", $con);

$result = mysql_query("SELECT group_id,name FROM groups where (group_id in (select
group_id from members where userid='$_GET[userid]') or group_id=0) order by name" );

echo "<records>";

while($row = mysql_fetch_array($result))
{
  echo "<record>";
  echo "<group_id>" . $row['group_id'] . "</group_id>" . "<name>" . $row['name'] . "</name>";
  echo "</record>";
}

echo "</records>";

mysql_close($con);
?>
```

groups_update.php

This code will take the userid, group name and security code of a group as input and 1) if the group already exists and the security code matches the group will add the user as a valid user of that group, or 2) if the group doesn't currently exist will create the group using the given security code and assign the user passed in as having access rights to that group.

```php
<?php
$con = mysql_connect("dalematheny.domaincommysql.com","damath","sites");
if (!$con)
  {
  die('Could not connect: ' . mysql_error());
  }

mysql_select_db("sites", $con);

   $result = mysql_query("SELECT group_id,name,code FROM groups where
name='$_GET[name]'");

   if ($row = mysql_fetch_array($result))  //group exists
   {
      $code=$row['code'];
      $group_id=$row['group_id'];
      if ($code==$_GET[code]) {
         $result = mysql_query("INSERT INTO members (group_id, userid) VALUES ($group_id,
'$_GET[userid]' )");
      }
      else {  // code doesn't match - exit with error
         $group_id=-1;
      }
   }
   else { //group doesn't exist so create it
      $result = mysql_query("INSERT INTO groups (name, code) VALUES ('$_GET[name]',
'$_GET[code]' )");
      $group_id=mysql_insert_id();
      $result = mysql_query("INSERT INTO members (group_id, userid) VALUES ($group_id,
'$_GET[userid]' )");
   }

echo "<records><record>";
echo "<group_id>" . $group_id . "</group_id>";
echo "</record></records>";

mysql_close($con);
?>
```

groups_delete.php

Pass in the group_id and security code and the code will delete the group and related members records if the code matches the one it was created with. The code returns an error condition of group_id=-1 if the security code doesn't match.

```php
<?php
$con = mysql_connect("dalematheny.domaincommysql.com","damath","sites");
if (!$con)
  {
  die('Could not connect: ' . mysql_error());
  }

mysql_select_db("sites", $con);


   $result = mysql_query("SELECT name,code,group_id FROM groups where
group_id='$_GET[group_id]'");

  if ($row = mysql_fetch_array($result))  //group exists
  {
     $code=$row['code'];
     $group_id=-1;
     if ($code==$_GET[code]) {
        $group_id=$row['group_id'];
        mysql_query("DELETE FROM groups WHERE group_id=$group_id");
        mysql_query("DELETE FROM members WHERE group_id=$group_id");
     }
  }

  //group_id=-1 is error: code doesn't match so no delete is done
  echo "<records><record>";
  echo "<group_id>" . $group_id . "</group_id>";
  echo "</record></records>";

mysql_close($con);
?>
```

Groups Coding Solution

You are encouraged to code the solution yourself before reading this section. If you wish to just follow through my solution then continue on and update *WebMarks* with the following code. The numbers below correspond to the coding design above.

Group Data access changes

Add the following code to our DataAccess.h file to support group and member creation and updates.

```
-(void)groupSelect :(id)obj;
-(void)groupInsert :(NSString *)groupName :(NSString *)groupCode :(id)obj;
-(void)groupDelete:(int)group_id :(NSString *)groupCode :(id)obj;

@end
```

Select groups data access code is shown below. Insert this line at the top of DataAccess.m:

```
#import "Groups.h"

@implementation DataAccess
Sites *sitesDelegate;
Groups *groupsDelegate;
```

The code should be inserted at the bottom of the DataAccess.m file and calls the PHP script.

```
/***************** GROUPS DATA SUPPORT ****************************/
/***************** GROUPS DATA SUPPORT ****************************/
/***************** GROUPS DATA SUPPORT ****************************/

-(void)parseGroupData:(NSData *)data {
    //Prepare parsing of xml.
    NSString *astr = [[NSString alloc] initWithData:data
encoding:NSWindowsCP1252StringEncoding];
    NSLog(@"Data:%@",astr);

    NSMutableArray *linksarray=[NSMutableArray new];
    CXMLDocument *doc = [[CXMLDocument alloc] initWithData:data options:0 error:nil];
    NSString *aname=@"";

    NSDictionary *row1;
    NSArray *nodes = [doc nodesForXPath:@"//record" error:nil];
    for (CXMLElement *node in nodes) {
        if ([node childCount]>1)
            aname=[[node childAtIndex:1] stringValue];

        row1=[[NSDictionary alloc] initWithObjectsAndKeys:
            [NSNumber numberWithInt:[[[node childAtIndex:0] stringValue]
integerValue]],@"group_id",
            aname, @"name", nil];
```

```
      [linksarray addObject:row1];
    }
    [groupsDelegate reLoadSites:linksarray];
}

-(void)groupSelect :(id)obj
{
    groupsDelegate=obj;
    NSString *userid=[UIDevice currentDevice].identifierForVendor.UUIDString;
    NSString *requestString = [NSString
stringWithFormat:@"http://rayoflightsoftware.com/sites/groups_get_children.php?userid=%@",us
erid];
    [self GetDataToParse:requestString :@"parseGroupData:" :self];
}
```

New or Access existing Group

```
-(void)groupInsertResponse:(NSData *)data {
    CXMLDocument *doc = [[CXMLDocument alloc] initWithData:data options:0 error:nil];
    NSArray *nodes = [doc nodesForXPath:@"//record" error:nil];
    CXMLElement *node=[nodes objectAtIndex:0];
    int group_id=[[[node childAtIndex:0] stringValue] integerValue];
    if (group_id==-1) {
        [groupsDelegate groupError:@"Invalid code on attempt to access existing group."];
    }
    else {
        [self groupSelect:groupsDelegate];
    }
}

-(void)groupInsert:(NSString *)groupName :(NSString *)groupCode :(id)obj
{
    groupsDelegate=obj;
    NSString *userid=[UIDevice currentDevice].identifierForVendor.UUIDString;
    NSString *requestString = [NSString
stringWithFormat:@"http://rayoflightsoftware.com/sites/groups_update.php?name=%@&code=%
@&userid=%@",groupName,groupCode,userid];
    requestString=[requestString stringByReplacingOccurrencesOfString:@" " withString:@"+"];

    [self GetDataToParse:requestString :@"groupInsertResponse:" :self];
}
```

Delete Group

```
-(void)groupDeleteResponse:(NSData *)data {
    CXMLDocument *doc = [[CXMLDocument alloc] initWithData:data options:0 error:nil];
    NSArray *nodes = [doc nodesForXPath:@"//record" error:nil];
    CXMLElement *node=[nodes objectAtIndex:0];
    int group_id=[[[node childAtIndex:0] stringValue] integerValue];
    if (group_id==-1) {
```

```
        [groupsDelegate groupError:@"Invalid code on attempt to delete group."];
      }
      else {
        [self groupSelect:groupsDelegate];
      }
}

-(void)groupDelete:(int)group_id :(NSString *)groupCode :(id)obj
{
    groupsDelegate=obj;
    NSString *requestString = [NSString
stringWithFormat:@"http://rayoflightsoftware.com/sites/groups_delete.php?group_id=%d&code=
%@",group_id,groupCode];
    [self GetDataToParse:requestString :@"groupDeleteResponse:" :self];
}
```

WebMarks screen changes to select a group

The following change to appDelegate, our global application object, allows us to save the current group we selected at a global scope so that we can access it anywhere in the app—specifically, from our Browser screen (which is the viewer object). We do this so that when we add a WebMark from our Browser screen the website will be saved to our currently selected group.

Within AppDelegate.h add the following group variable declaration:

```
@interface AppDelegate : UIResponder <UIApplicationDelegate>
{
    NSNumber *cur_group;
}
@property (strong, nonatomic) NSNumber *cur_group;
```

In sites.h, add:

```
    int curGroup;
    NSString *currentGroup;

@property (nonatomic, retain) NSString *currentGroup;
-(void)setGroup :(int)agroup :(NSString *)groupname;
```

In sites.m add at the top:

```
#import "Groups.h"
#import "AppDelegate.h"

@implementation Sites
@synthesize default_site, sitesData, currentGroup;
```

Insert this function above viewDidLoad. It will set our current group values including the one in our AppDelegate application-level object:

```
-(void)setGroupValues:(int)agroup :(NSString *)groupname {
    curGroup=agroup;
    currentGroup=groupname;
    AppDelegate *appDelegate = [[UIApplication sharedApplication] delegate];
    appDelegate.cur_group=[NSNumber numberWithInt:curGroup];
}
```

Add the following to the *ViewDidLoad* method:

```
    self.navigationItem.rightBarButtonItem = self.editButtonItem;
    [self setGroupValues:0 :@"Global"];
    self.navigationItem.leftBarButtonItem = [[UIBarButtonItem alloc]initWithTitle:@"Groups"
style:UIBarButtonItemStylePlain target:self action:@selector(doGroups:)];
```

Add the methods below to sites.m to handle to user touching the "Groups" button to create the group screen as well as handle setting a new group as the current group when the user returns from the Groups screen (the setGroup method does this).

```
-(IBAction)doGroups:(id)sender {
    Groups *controller = [[Groups alloc] initWithNibName:@"Groups" bundle:nil];
    controller.atab=self;
    [controller setGroupid:curGroup];
    [self.navigationController pushViewController:controller animated:YES];
}

-(void)refreshGroupDisplay {
    [aData sitesLoad:self.sitesData :curGroup :self];
    [self.tableView reloadData];
}

-(void)setGroup :(int)agroup :(NSString *)groupname {
    [self setGroupValues:agroup :groupname];
    [self refreshGroupDisplay];
}
```

Add to the top of *viewDidAppear* method:
```
    self.title=[NSString stringWithFormat:@"WebMarks:%@",currentGroup];
```

and modify in the same routine:

```
    [aData sitesLoad:self.sitesData :0 :self];
    [self.tableView reloadData];
```
to
```
    [self refreshGroupDisplay];
```

An within the *setValue* method, update the *sitesInsertUpdate* call to pass *curGroup* instead of 0:

```
-(void)setValue :(NSString *)aname :(NSString *)asite :(int)rank :(int)group_id :(int)arow
:(NSString *)attr {
. . .
site_id=[aData sitesInsertUpdate:aname :asite :site_id :rank :curGroup :attr :self];
    [self updateSiteid:site_id];
```

 The logic below will allow the viewer object (Browser screen) to bookmark websites into the current group as given by our global AppDelegate variable: cur_group.

Within viewer.m add the import at the top:

```
#import "AppDelegate.h"
```

And then modify the addAction method as follows. Replace the line:

```
int site_id=[aData1 sitesInsertUpdate:theTitle :currentUrl :0 :0 :0 :@"" :self];
```

With:

```
AppDelegate *appDelegate = [[UIApplication sharedApplication] delegate];
int group_id=[appDelegate.cur_group intValue];
int site_id=[aData1 sitesInsertUpdate:theTitle :currentUrl :0 :0 :group_id :@"" :self];
```

Update Detail screen

 From the Detail.xib screen, remove the picker control and "Owner" label. Remove the following code from the Detail.h file:

```
NSArray *_pickerdata;
@property (weak, nonatomic) IBOutlet UIPickerView *picker;
@property (nonatomic, retain) NSArray *_pickerdata;
```

Remove from the Detail.m file:
```
@synthesize _pickerdata, picker;
```

From viewDidLoad, remove:
```
_pickerdata = @[@"Everyone", @"Myself", @"Group A", @"Group B", @"Group C", @"Group D"];
```

Remove the picker code at the bottom:
```
-(void)viewDidAppear:(BOOL)animated {
    [picker selectRow:site_group_id inComponent:0 animated:YES];
}

- (int)numberOfComponentsInPickerView:(UIPickerView *)pickerView
{
    return 1;
}

- (int)pickerView:(UIPickerView *)pickerView numberOfRowsInComponent:(NSInteger)component
{
    return _pickerdata.count;
}

// The data to return for the row and component (column) that's being passed in
- (NSString*)pickerView:(UIPickerView *)pickerView titleForRow:(NSInteger)row
forComponent:(NSInteger)component
{
    return _pickerdata[row];
}

// Catpure the picker view selection
- (void)pickerView:(UIPickerView *)pickerView didSelectRow:(NSInteger)row
inComponent:(NSInteger)component
{
    // This method is triggered whenever the user makes a change to the picker selection.
    // The parameter named row and component represents what was selected.
    site_group_id=row;
}
```

New Groups Screen

 Create a new Groups screen with .xib file as type: *UITableViewController*.
The code follows that handles all steps above: a through f. Code for Groups.h:

```objc
#import <UIKit/UIKit.h>
#import "Sites.h"

@interface Groups : UITableViewController
{
   int curGroup_id;
   NSMutableArray *groupData;
   Sites *atab;
   NSString *curGroup;
}

@property (nonatomic, retain) NSString *curGroup;
@property (nonatomic, retain) Sites *atab;
@property (nonatomic,strong) NSMutableArray * groupData;
- (void)reLoadSites :(NSMutableArray *)sitesArray;
-(void)setGroupid :(int)agroupid;
-(void)groupError:(NSString *)errorStr;
@end
```

And code for Groups.m:

```objc
#import "Groups.h"
#import "DataAccess.h"

@implementation Groups
@synthesize groupData, atab, curGroup;
DataAccess *aData2;

-(void)setGroupid :(int)agroupid {
   curGroup_id=agroupid;
}

- (void)viewDidLoad {
   [super viewDidLoad];
   self.title=@"WebMark Groups";
   aData2 = [[DataAccess alloc] init];
   self.navigationItem.rightBarButtonItem = [[UIBarButtonItem alloc]
initWithBarButtonSystemItem:UIBarButtonSystemItemAdd target:self
action:@selector(addAction:)];
   [aData2 groupSelect:self];
}

-(void)viewDidDisappear:(BOOL)animated {
   [atab setGroup:curGroup_id :curGroup];
}
```

```objc
-(IBAction)addAction:(id)sender {
   UIAlertController * alert= [UIAlertController
                      alertControllerWithTitle:@"Add Group"
                      message:@"Enter Group Name and Security Code to either create a new
group or add yourself as a member of the group."
                      preferredStyle:UIAlertControllerStyleAlert];
   UIAlertAction* ok = [UIAlertAction actionWithTitle:@"OK" style:UIAlertActionStyleDefault
                             handler:^(UIAlertAction * action) {
                          NSString *groupname = ((UITextField *)[alert.textFields
objectAtIndex:0]).text;
                          NSString *groupcode = ((UITextField *)[alert.textFields
objectAtIndex:1]).text;

                          [aData2 groupInsert:groupname :groupcode :self];
                          [alert dismissViewControllerAnimated:YES completion:nil];
                       }];
   UIAlertAction* cancel = [UIAlertAction actionWithTitle:@"Cancel"
style:UIAlertActionStyleDefault

                             handler:^(UIAlertAction * action) {
                          [alert dismissViewControllerAnimated:YES completion:nil];
                       }];


   [alert addAction:ok];
   [alert addAction:cancel];

   [alert addTextFieldWithConfigurationHandler:^(UITextField *textField) {
      textField.placeholder = @"Group Name";
   }];
   [alert addTextFieldWithConfigurationHandler:^(UITextField *textField) {
      textField.placeholder = @"Security Code";
      textField.secureTextEntry = YES;
   }];

   [self presentViewController:alert animated:YES completion:nil];
}

- (void)reLoadSites :(NSMutableArray *)sitesArray {
   if (groupData!=nil) {
      if (self.groupData!=nil) {
         [self.groupData removeAllObjects];
         groupData=nil;
      }
   }
   groupData=sitesArray;
   [self.tableView reloadData];
}

-(void)groupError:(NSString *)errorStr {
   UIAlertController * alert= [UIAlertController
                      alertControllerWithTitle:@"Group Error"
                      message:errorStr
                      preferredStyle:UIAlertControllerStyleAlert];
   UIAlertAction* ok = [UIAlertAction actionWithTitle:@"OK" style:UIAlertActionStyleDefault
                             handler:^(UIAlertAction * action) {
```

```
                                          [alert dismissViewControllerAnimated:YES completion:nil];
                      }];

    [alert addAction:ok];
    [self presentViewController:alert animated:YES completion:nil];
    [self.tableView reloadData];
}
```

TableView: Display and Select row

```
#pragma mark - Table view data source

- (NSInteger)numberOfSectionsInTableView:(UITableView *)tableView {
#warning Potentially incomplete method implementation.
    // Return the number of sections.
    return 1;
}

- (NSInteger)tableView:(UITableView *)tableView numberOfRowsInSection:(NSInteger)section {
#warning Incomplete method implementation.
    // Return the number of rows in the section.
    return [groupData count];
}

- (UITableViewCell *)tableView:(UITableView *)tableView cellForRowAtIndexPath:(NSIndexPath
*)indexPath {
    static NSString *CellIdentifier = @"Cell";
    UITableViewCell *cell = [tableView dequeueReusableCellWithIdentifier:CellIdentifier];
    if (cell == nil) {
        cell = [[UITableViewCell alloc] initWithStyle:UITableViewCellStyleSubtitle
reuseIdentifier:CellIdentifier];
    }

    // Configure the cell
    int arow=indexPath.row;
    NSDictionary *rowdata = [self.groupData objectAtIndex:arow];
    NSString *astr=[rowdata objectForKey:@"name"];
    cell.textLabel.text = astr;
    if ([[rowdata objectForKey:@"group_id"] integerValue]==curGroup_id) {
        cell.accessoryType=UITableViewCellAccessoryCheckmark;
        curGroup=astr;
    }
    else
        cell.accessoryType=UITableViewCellAccessoryNone;

    return cell;
}

// Override to support deleting rows within the table view.
- (void)tableView:(UITableView *)tableView
commitEditingStyle:(UITableViewCellEditingStyle)editingStyle forRowAtIndexPath:(NSIndexPath
```

```
*)indexPath {
   if (editingStyle == UITableViewCellEditingStyleDelete) {
      // Delete the row from the data source
      int arow=indexPath.row;
      NSDictionary *rowdata = [self.groupData objectAtIndex:arow];
      int agroup_id=[[rowdata objectForKey:@"group_id"] integerValue];
      UIAlertController * alert=  [UIAlertController
                     alertControllerWithTitle:@"Delete Group"
                     message:@"Enter the group's security code to delete the group."
                     preferredStyle:UIAlertControllerStyleAlert];
      UIAlertAction* ok = [UIAlertAction
                  actionWithTitle:@"OK"
                  style:UIAlertActionStyleDefault
                  handler:^(UIAlertAction * action)
                  {
                     NSString *groupcode = ((UITextField *)[alert.textFields
objectAtIndex:0]).text;
                     [aData2 groupDelete:agroup_id :groupcode :self];
                     [alert dismissViewControllerAnimated:YES completion:nil];
                     [self.groupData removeObjectAtIndex:indexPath.row];
                     [tableView deleteRowsAtIndexPaths:@[indexPath]
withRowAnimation:UITableViewRowAnimationFade];
                  }];
      [alert addAction:ok]; // add action to uialertcontroller
      [alert addTextFieldWithConfigurationHandler:^(UITextField *textField) {
         textField.placeholder = @"Group Code";
      }];
      [self presentViewController:alert animated:YES completion:nil];
   } else if (editingStyle == UITableViewCellEditingStyleInsert) {
      // Create a new instance of the appropriate class, insert it into the array, and add a new row
to the table view
   }
}


// In a xib-based application, navigation from a table can be handled in -
tableView:didSelectRowAtIndexPath:
- (void)tableView:(UITableView *)tableView didSelectRowAtIndexPath:(NSIndexPath *)indexPath
{
   // Navigation logic may go here, for example:
   int arow=indexPath.row;
   NSDictionary *rowdata = [self.groupData objectAtIndex:arow];
   curGroup_id=[[rowdata objectForKey:@"group_id"] integerValue];
   curGroup=[rowdata objectForKey:@"name"];
   [self.tableView reloadData];
}

@end
```

Run the code and you should see "Groups" in the WebMarks screen. Tap this and try adding and selecting Groups and adding websites to each group.

Chapter 12: Social Sharing

We can use iOS provided libraries to share links with other people over the web. Specifically, we show Email, Facebook, and Twitter integration which will be accessed through the navigational tool of "Action Sheets." Action Sheets provide a menu of choices to a user when a website is tapped in the Sites screen.

 First, refer to a previous section on adding libraries to our project to add the libraries: **MessageUI.framework**, for eMail support, and **Social.framework**, for *Facebook* and *Twitter* support. The libraries screen should appear as the following when done:

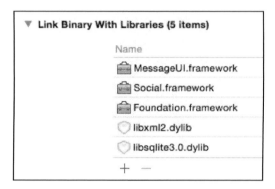

 You will need to add the following imports to the Sites.h file and the delegates to the *@interface Sites:* code.

```
#import <UIKit/UIKit.h>
#import "DataAccess.h"
#import <MessageUI/MessageUI.h>
#import <Social/Social.h>

@interface Sites : UITableViewController <UIActionSheetDelegate,
MFMailComposeViewControllerDelegate>
```

Action Sheets

Action sheets provide a navigational aid that displays a list of actions on the screen for the user to pick from. It is basically a dynamic menu function. See the picture to the right to see the Action Sheet we will be building in WebMarks.

 Replace the code in the *accessoryButtonTappedForRowWithIndexPath* method with the following which will call an action sheet to allow the user to pick options when tapping the detail disclosure (i)> button that use to be attached to just the Detail edit screen.

```
-(void)tableView:(UITableView *)tableView
accessoryButtonTappedForRowWithIndexPath:(NSIndexPath *)indexPath
{
   NSUInteger row = [indexPath row];
   NSDictionary *rowdata = [self.sitesData objectAtIndex:row];
   if ((!tableView.isEditing) || (row<[self.sitesData count])) {
     //This logic gets the current row from the sites array

     UIAlertController * alert= [UIAlertController
                      alertControllerWithTitle:@"Site Actions"
                      message:@"Select an action to perform on selected website."
                      preferredStyle:UIAlertControllerStyleActionSheet];

     UIAlertAction* detailEdit = [UIAlertAction
                     actionWithTitle:@"Edit Detail"
                     style:UIAlertActionStyleDefault
                     handler:^(UIAlertAction * action)
                     {
                        //These code lines put the current website row's data into variables
                        //that will be passed to the Detail screen.
                        int site_id=[[rowdata objectForKey:@"id"] integerValue];
                        int rank=[[rowdata objectForKey:@"rank"] integerValue];
                        int group_id=[[rowdata objectForKey:@"group_id"] integerValue];
                        NSString *name=[rowdata objectForKey:@"name"];
                        NSString *attr=[rowdata objectForKey:@"attributes"];

                        //create Detail screen
                        Detail *detailview = [[Detail alloc] initWithNibName:@"Detail" bundle:nil];
                        detailview.site_name=name;
                        detailview.atab=self;
                        [detailview setValue:site_id :row :rank :group_id :[rowdata
objectForKey:@"site"] :attr];
                        [self.navigationController pushViewController:detailview animated:YES];
                        [alert dismissViewControllerAnimated:YES completion:nil];
                     }];


     UIAlertAction* email = [UIAlertAction
                     actionWithTitle:@"Email"
                     style:UIAlertActionStyleDefault
                     handler:^(UIAlertAction * action)
                     {
                        [self doSendEmail];
                        [alert dismissViewControllerAnimated:YES completion:nil];
                     }];

     UIAlertAction* facebook = [UIAlertAction
                     actionWithTitle:@"Post to Facebook"
                     style:UIAlertActionStyleDefault
                     handler:^(UIAlertAction * action)
                     {
                        [self postToFacebook];
                        [alert dismissViewControllerAnimated:YES completion:nil];
```

113

```
                    }];

    UIAlertAction* twitter = [UIAlertAction
                    actionWithTitle:@"Post to Twitter"
                    style:UIAlertActionStyleDefault
                    handler:^(UIAlertAction * action)
                    {
                        [self postToTwitter];
                        [alert dismissViewControllerAnimated:YES completion:nil];
                    }];

    UIAlertAction* cancel = [UIAlertAction
                    actionWithTitle:@"Cancel"
                    style:UIAlertActionStyleDefault
                    handler:^(UIAlertAction * action)
                    {
                        [alert dismissViewControllerAnimated:YES completion:nil];
                    }];

    [alert addAction:detailEdit]; // add action to uialertcontroller
    [alert addAction:email]; // add action to uialertcontroller
    [alert addAction:facebook]; // add action to uialertcontroller
    [alert addAction:twitter]; // add action to uialertcontroller
    [alert addAction:cancel]; // add action to uialertcontroller
    alert.popoverPresentationController.sourceView = self.view;
    alert.popoverPresentationController.sourceRect =
CGRectMake((self.view.bounds.size.width / 2.0)-150, (self.view.bounds.size.height / 2.0)-150,
1.0, 1.0);
    [self presentViewController:alert animated:YES completion:nil];
    }
}
```

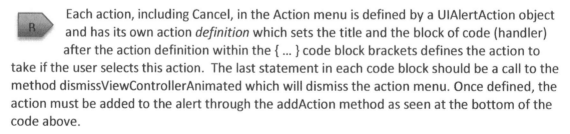

UIAlertController with parameter *preferredStyle:UIAlertControllerStyleActionSheet* sets up the Action Sheet with a title and message that show on top.

Each action, including Cancel, in the Action menu is defined by a UIAlertAction object and has its own action *definition* which sets the title and the block of code (handler) after the action definition within the { ... } code block brackets defines the action to take if the user selects this action. The last statement in each code block should be a call to the method dismissViewControllerAnimated which will dismiss the action menu. Once defined, the action must be added to the alert through the addAction method as seen at the bottom of the code above.

The *presentViewController* presents the alert. Note the two lines of code above this statement support iPad formatting of this action menu.

Email Integration

Add the following code to Sites.m at the end of the file before "@end". The logic will allow the user to send an email screen with the selected website name and URL.

```objc
-(void)doSendEmail {
    NSDateFormatter *dateFormat = [[NSDateFormatter alloc] init];
    [dateFormat setDateFormat:@"MMM d yyyy"];
    NSString *adate = [dateFormat stringFromDate:[[NSDate alloc] init]];

    NSDictionary *rowdata = [self.sitesData objectAtIndex:curRow];
    NSString *name=[rowdata objectForKey:@"name"];
    NSString *site=[rowdata objectForKey:@"site"];
    NSString *amsg=[NSString stringWithFormat:@"Check out this cool site named:%@. %@
Message sent at date:%@",name,site,adate];

    if ([MFMailComposeViewController canSendMail])
    {
        MFMailComposeViewController *mail = [[MFMailComposeViewController alloc] init];
        mail.mailComposeDelegate = self;
        [mail setSubject:@"Send Link"];
        [mail setMessageBody:amsg isHTML:NO];

        [self presentViewController:mail animated:YES completion:NULL];
    }
    else
    {
        NSLog(@"This device cannot send email");
    }
}

// This controller gets called when user takes an action on the email.  Logic can be added as
desired to respond to the result if desired.

- (void)mailComposeController:(MFMailComposeViewController*)controller
        didFinishWithResult:(MFMailComposeResult)result
                error:(NSError*)error;
{
    switch (result) {
        case MFMailComposeResultSent:
            NSLog(@"You sent the email.");
            break;
        case MFMailComposeResultSaved:
            NSLog(@"You saved a draft of this email");
            break;
        case MFMailComposeResultCancelled:
            NSLog(@"You cancelled sending this email.");
            break;
        case MFMailComposeResultFailed:
            NSLog(@"Mail failed:  An error occurred when trying to compose this email");
            break;
        default:
```

```
        NSLog(@"An error occurred when trying to compose this email");
        break;
    }
    [self dismissViewControllerAnimated:YES completion:NULL];
}
```

 This code creates a string *adate* using the current date and the given format "MMM d yyyy" which is like 'Jan 20, 2015' Other date formats are available.

 This code sets up the subject and message of the email. *presentViewController* method displays the email to the user where they can add receipients and send it.

Twitter Integration

Native Twitter integration is part of the iOS social framework library. Note that you must have a Twitter account configured on your device for this code to work (see the function *isAvailableForServiceType* in the code that checks for this condition).

 Add the following code to Sites.m at the end of the file before "@end" to send a tweet from the sample app.

```
- (void)postToTwitter {
    if ([SLComposeViewController isAvailableForServiceType:SLServiceTypeTwitter])
    {
        SLComposeViewController *tweetSheet = [SLComposeViewController
composeViewControllerForServiceType:SLServiceTypeTwitter];

        NSDictionary *rowdata = [self.sitesData objectAtIndex:curRow];
        NSString *name=[rowdata objectForKey:@"name"];
        NSString *site=[rowdata objectForKey:@"site"];
        NSString *amsg=[NSString stringWithFormat:@"Check out this cool site named:%@.
%@",name,site];

        [tweetSheet setInitialText:amsg];
        [self presentViewController:tweetSheet animated:YES completion:nil];
    }
}
```

Facebook Integration

Native Facebook integration is part of the iOS social framework library. Note that you must have a Facebook account configured on your device for this code to work (see the function *isAvailableForServiceType* in the code that checks for this condition).

Add the following code to Sites.m at the end of the file before "@end" to send a Facebook post from the sample app.

```objc
- (void)postToFacebook {
    if([SLComposeViewController isAvailableForServiceType:SLServiceTypeFacebook]) {

        SLComposeViewController *controller = [SLComposeViewController composeViewControllerForServiceType:SLServiceTypeFacebook];

        NSDictionary *rowdata = [self.sitesData objectAtIndex:curRow];
        NSString *name=[rowdata objectForKey:@"name"];
        NSString *site=[rowdata objectForKey:@"site"];
        NSString *amsg=[NSString stringWithFormat:@"Check out this cool site %@",name];

        [controller setInitialText:amsg];
        [controller addURL:[NSURL URLWithString:site]];
        // following code would add an image as well
        // [controller addImage:[UIImage imageNamed:@"socialsharing-facebook-image.jpg"]];

        [self presentViewController:controller animated:YES completion:Nil];
    }
}
```

Run the app and click on a website then choose all three options: eMail, Facebook, and Twitter.

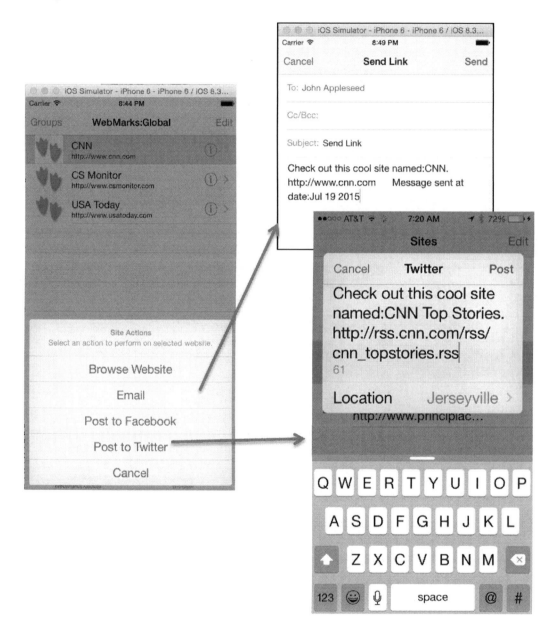

Chapter 13: Adding ads to your app

Even though WebMarks is a free app, we can add ads to the app and make money for every display of the ad. With iAds in the header of our WebMarks view the app looks like the image on the right.

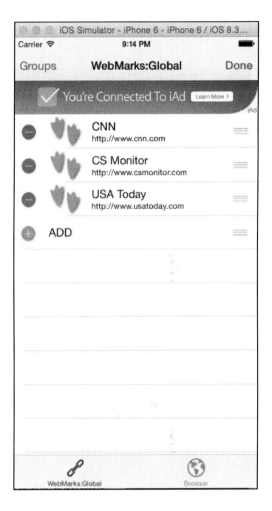

Apple provides the ads and all we have to do is provide the following code in the sites screen and ads will appear as in the image to the left. These ads bring in about $.02 per downloaded app—or about $10 per 500 downloads. Many factors, such as how often users click through your ads, can change this amount but it can be a nice way to make some money off of an app.

Adding code for iAds is easy. First you must add the iAd framework by clicking on the WebMarks application name at the top of your file list in XCode and then tap on the tab: Build Phases and go to "Link Binary with Libraries" section and press add ("+") button add search for iAd and add it. Your library list should now be like this:

2 Within sites.h add the following:

```
#import <iAd/iAd.h>

@interface Sites : UITableViewController <UIActionSheetDelegate,
MFMailComposeViewControllerDelegate, ADBannerViewDelegate>
{
   BOOL _bannerIsVisible;
   ADBannerView *_adBanner;


   . . .

@property (nonatomic, strong) ADBannerView *_adBanner;
```

Within sites.m add the following at the top:
```
@synthesize _adBanner;
```

and add to the top of *viewDidLoad* method:
```
- (void)viewDidLoad {
   [super viewDidLoad];
   _adBanner = [[ADBannerView alloc] initWithFrame:CGRectMake(0, 0, 320, 50)];
   _adBanner.delegate = self;
```

and add to the bottom of sites.m. This adds the banner view: _adBanner as the footer of our tableView.
```
- (void)bannerViewDidLoadAd:(ADBannerView *)banner
{
   if (!_bannerIsVisible)
   {
      // If banner isn't part of view hierarchy, add it
      if (_adBanner.superview == nil)
         self.tableView.tableHeaderView = _adBanner;
      [UIView beginAnimations:@"animateAdBannerOn" context:NULL];
      [UIView commitAnimations];
      _bannerIsVisible = YES;
   }
}

- (void)bannerView:(ADBannerView *)banner didFailToReceiveAdWithError: (NSError *)error
{
   if (_bannerIsVisible)
   {
      [UIView beginAnimations:@"animateAdBannerOff" context:NULL];
      [UIView commitAnimations];
      _bannerIsVisible = NO;
   }
}
```

Chapter 14: Submitting Apps to the App Store

Preparing and app for submission and submitting the app require a number of steps:

- Registering as an Apple Developer—and a related $99 charge per year.
- Code Signing your app
- Testing on devices
- App icons and images
- Creating an online profile of your app
- Creating the Archive build and uploading your app for review

This section outlines these steps and illustrates the process with the Sites app as it was submitted to the App Store.

Registering as an Apple Developer

While XCode development environment is free, to distribute an app on the app store requires a $99/year developer membership. Go to the Apple Developer site at and sign up! The site is:

https://developer.apple.com/

Code signing, Certificates, Provisioning files

To release an app or test on real devices there is an involved process of creating a developer and distribution certificates, an app ID, registration of devices to test with and provisioning files. These are all available within the Apple Developer Member Center.

The basic process to to create both developer and distribution certificates, then create an App ID. The most important part of the app id is the bundle ID must match the bundle identifier in your app. So the following screen shows the bundle identifier in XCode by clicking on the App name and going to "Info". Make sure this is the same as what you type for "Explicit App ID" when creating the App ID through the Apple Developer member center. Screens shots for both follow:

Xcode Info screen for the app:

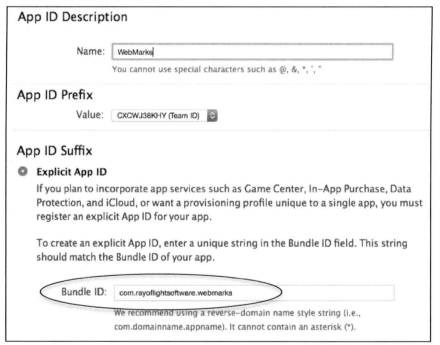

From App ID creation from the Member Center:

App ID Description

Name: WebMarks

You cannot use special characters such as @, &, *, ', "

App ID Prefix

Value: CXCWJ38KHY (Team ID)

App ID Suffix

⦿ **Explicit App ID**

If you plan to incorporate app services such as Game Center, In-App Purchase, Data Protection, and iCloud, or want a provisioning profile unique to a single app, you must register an explicit App ID for your app.

To create an explicit App ID, enter a unique string in the Bundle ID field. This string should match the Bundle ID of your app.

Bundle ID: com.rayoflightsoftware.webmarks

We recommend using a reverse-domain name style string (i.e., com.domainname.appname). It cannot contain an asterisk (*).

After the app ID is created you will need to register devices for testing online and then create both development and distribution provisions files. Provisions files, after created, are downloaded and double-clicked on your Mac to register them with XCode. They are then available to set in the provisioning profile of the **Code Signing** settings found under the system **Build Setting** tab. See example below where the "WebMarks Dev" profile was selected.

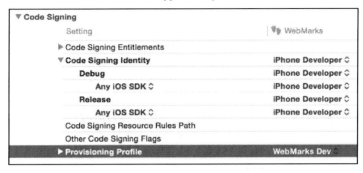

See the online documentation on each of these steps from Apple on the Member Center but also know there are many online tutorials that can also help with this process.

Testing on devices

Before releasing you need to test on a real iPhone or iPad as the simulator cannot be relied on completely—nothing substitutes the real deal. There may also be some slight differences in execution and formatting.

To test, plug your iPhone into your development computer using your USB cable. The device should be registered as a valid device in your development provisioning profile mentioned above. At the top of XCode, in the devices list you've used when running the simulator you'll see your device. Example image below shows my iPhone hooked up.

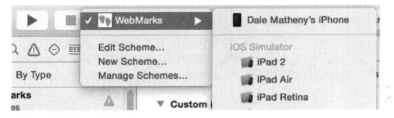

Select the device and then press RUN and XCode will prepare your device for development and then transfer the app to the device and run it. The great thing is that you can debug in XCode while running on the device—very handy. You can also now disconnect your device and use your app on your iPhone or iPad—very cool!

App Icons and Images

In the project folder click on the file ***images.xcassets***. This shows the dozen icon files of various sizes that you need to support various versions of iOS devices. There is a very cool online app at http://makeappicon.com/# where you insert a 1024x1024 pixel image of your icon and it generates the dozen images of all appropriate sizes you need for your app. Use this tool and download the resulting images and drag-n-drop them into the appropriate spot on this form. The final version for the WebMarks app is shown below.

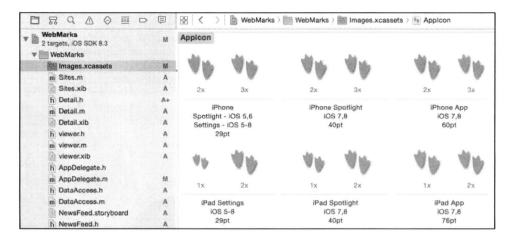

Creating an online profile of your app

To create a profile of your app for submission to Apple, within the Apple Developer Member Center log into ITunes Connect—this is the management area for your apps. Select "My Apps" and then press the "+" key to create a new iOS app. You will key in the name of the app and can select your own SKU (0005 below), and enter the Bundle ID we created above when creating the App ID. The screen should appear as the following – press Create.

Click on the new App Icon on you're my Apps screen and fill in all of the information asked for. Samples from WebMarks appear below. There are also screenshots required which can be taken from the simulator by pressing Command-S on your keyboard. The screenshots will appear as .png files on your desktop. Note that you will need a website URL for users to go to for support for the app. See the one page website I created for WebMarks at www.rayoflightsoftware.com/WebMarks

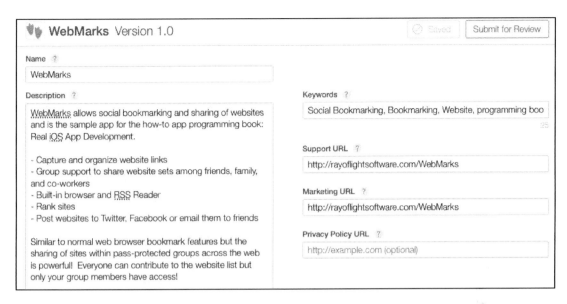

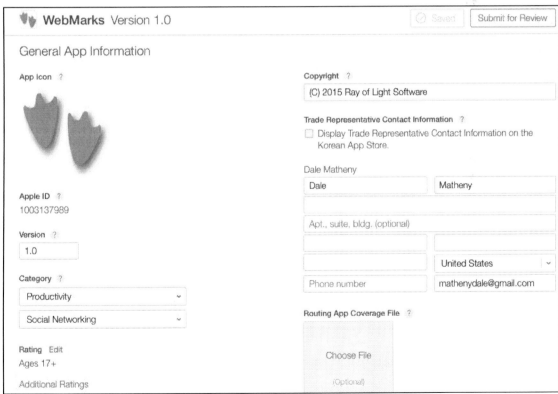

At the top of the App definition screen select Pricing to get the following screen to set your pricing for the app.

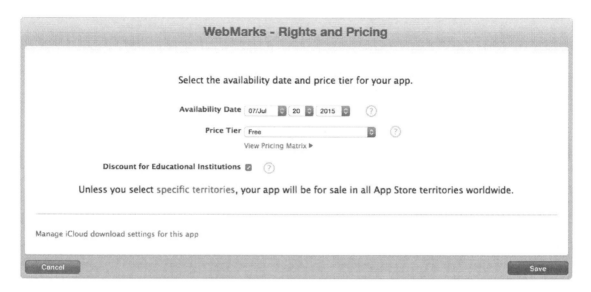

Creating the Archive build and uploading your app for review

The next to the last step (before releasing the app after review) is to create an Archive version of the application and upload it to iTunes Connect. To do this within XCode:

1. Select the menu item Product / Clean
2. Select the menu item Product / Archive and wait. Answer any questions or resolve code signing issues.
3. From the *Organizer* screen (shown below) click on the WebMarks archive you just created and click on "Submit to App Store…". If all is well your file will be validated and uploaded.

4. Now to go to the App description within the iTunes Connect system using your web browser. If you scroll down to the Build section you need to tap here and select the version you just uploaded.

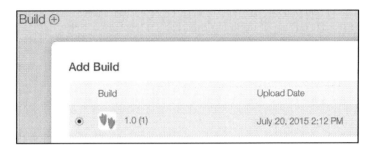

5. Now click **Save** and **"Submit for Review"** buttons at the top of the form.

You're all set! Review takes about one week and may be rejected if anything in your code accesses more on the iOS device than it should. When it passes muster then you can release the app to the App Store!

Additional Exercises

The following exercises give additional challenges and practice is your app building. Note that browsing Google using the keyword "XCode" and other related words is invaluable for finding answers to how to code some of the exercises below and other features you wish to add to your own apps.

1. Add logic when a website is created through the detail screen to add 'http://' or 'www.' if it is left off of a site name.

2. When the bookmark is tapped, '+' symbol on Browser screen, add logic to ask what group it should be placed in. Right now all new websites are placed in the global group.

3. Add a screen to enter parameters that manage formatting such as sort order for display of websites. Save the parameters in the database in a new parameters table in the local SQLite database and reload them on start-up.

4. Store the image selected on the detail screen. See file management so you can store the image in the local file sandbox.

5. Add a function to take a screen capture of the website in the browser and store it as the image related to the website.

6. Import bookmarks from the Safari browser (see Bookmarks.plist).

INDEX

ABOUT THE AUTHOR

Dale Matheny is an Assistant Professor at Principia College where he teaches Business Administration including Business Analytics, Operations, and App Development. He is an Apple Developer and owns Ray of Light Software, a small mobile app development company and has published four apps to the App Store. He has spent 25 years as a consultant, manager, software architect and product manager in the computer software industry. Dale has consulted internationally on business analytics at Fortune 500 companies.